W9-AQN-914

THE
BOTTOM
OF THE
SEA
AND
BEYOND

Also by Carl Heintze
Circle of Fire: The Great Chain of Volcanoes and Earth Faults
Genetic Engineering: Man and Nature in Transition
A Million Locks and Keys
The Priceless Pump
Search Among the Stars

The Bottom of the Sea and Beyond

by
Carl Heintze

THOMAS NELSON INC., PUBLISHERS
Nashville   New York

ST. PHILIPS COLLEGE LIBRARY

551.4608
H471

Copyright © 1975 by Carl Heintze

All rights reserved under International and Pan-American Conven-
tions. Published in Nashville, Tennessee, by Thomas Nelson, Inc.,
and simultaneously in Don Mills, Ontario, by Thomas Nelson &
Sons (Canada) Limited. Manufactured in the United States of
America.

First edition

The map on page 98 has been reprinted by permission from TIME,
The Weekly Newsmagazine, Copyright Time Inc.

Library of Congress Cataloging in Publication Data
Heintze, Carl.
   The bottom of the sea and beyond.
   Bibliography: p.
   SUMMARY: Briefly discusses the history of oceanography and de-
scribes what recent oceanographic studies have revealed about the ocean
floor and the earth's interior beneath it.
   1. Submarine geology.   2. Ocean bottom.
[1. Ocean bottom. 2. Oceanography. 3. Geology] I. Title.
QE39.H42   551.4'608   74-34393
ISBN 0-8407-6432-4

In memory of

Michael Cash,

1954–1974,

who loved

the sea

41521

Contents:

Chapter 1

TOUCHING
BOTTOM

If, one day in 1972, you had been traveling by tramp steamer from Puget Sound in Washington south to San Francisco along the Pacific Coast, you might have seen a strange vessel, apparently anchored off the starboard side of your ship. Most of its deck would have appeared flat, and its superstructure would have been located aft, much like that of an oil tanker. But this ship would have looked like no tanker afloat.

If your vessel passed close enough to the ship, you would have been able to read its name, the *Glomar Challenger,* on the bow and stern. Centered on the main deck of the *Glomar Challenger* would have been what seemed to be an oil-drilling rig, so that you might have guessed it was drilling for oil. That would have been incorrect, too. The *Glomar Challenger* was indeed drilling, but not for oil.

9

ST. PHILIPS COLLEGE LIBRARY

A long linked line of pipe, called a *drill string,* extended from the drilling rig through a special well in the center of the ship, down through several thousand feet of water into the bottom of the sea. The *Glomar Challenger* was especially designed to probe into the sea floor to unlock its secrets and bring them to the surface.

The *Glomar Challenger* is one of the latest and most powerful tools devised by scientists to examine the least known and largest of the earth's physical frontiers, the bottom of the sea. Although science has discovered many things about our planet, it still knows very little about this part of the earth. The flights of the Apollo astronauts, the journeys of the Russian lunar landers, and the mapping expeditions of lunar satellites and space probes to Mars have given science a much better picture of the surface of our two neighbors in space than we have of our own planet. That is because three fourths of the earth's surface is covered with water and hidden from man's direct examination.

Alone among the nine planets of the solar system, the earth possesses a vast ocean surface. It also contains more water than any other planet. Indeed, it is a water-soaked world. Not only does water cover most of the earth, water vapor in the form of clouds also hides the surface of the earth's continents from space. An alien from another world, approaching the earth, would see it as a mottled white-and-bluish-green ball. He would have to be very close to it before he could see the outlines of the continents and almost upon its surface before he could make out signs of man's alteration of the earth's natural waterways with such projects as the Panama and Suez canals.

A port-side view of the Deep Sea Drilling Project vessel, *Glomar Challenger*, which is drilling and coring for ocean sediment in all the oceans of the world. The 10,400-ton ship is 400 feet long, and the 142-foot-tall drilling derrick has a hook-load capacity of 1 million pounds. *Courtesy Scripps Institution of Oceanography*

Even if our alien visitor were to land, he would, like us, be unable to see that portion of the earth's crust that lies beneath the seas, because the surface of the sea reflects light. The molecules of water bounce back the rays of the sun into the atmosphere and space, creating great opaque patches where the seas lie. Our visitor from another planet might even think the oceans were land surface, just as early astronomers, used to the oceans, thought exactly the reverse of Mars and the moon. So used to water were they that they believed the plains of the moon were seas, and thought they saw canals on Mars. Today we know the moon's "oceans" were misnamed. They are not seas, but great dusty plains. Nor do the canals of Mars exist; they were optical illusions created by that planet's surface.

Like both the moon and Mars, however, the earth does have a single rigid outer layer, its crust. The crust is thicker where the continents stand and thinner beneath the seas. The continents are the part of this layer that we can see. They are, in fact, really islands in a single ocean that covers most of the earth. Only the fact that the earth is sufficiently cool to keep some of its water as ice in its polar ice caps prevents more of the land from being submerged.

We know a great deal about the continents. During man's history he has walked, ridden, and flown all over them, mapping them in great detail. Even in the Amazon Basin of South America and the Congo area of Central Africa, where dense vegetation covers everything, the general features of the land have been measured and charted with accuracy. The airplane and the space satellite have greatly improved man's ability to map the land surface of the earth. Airplanes have made photographic mapping possible, and military and civilian reconnaissance satellites give us daily pictures of large parts of the earth's surface.

From all these studies, scientists have come to believe that the earth beneath the sea is much like the portion above the oceans, yet they are not certain. The sea bottom is immense, perhaps 140 million square miles. It is far from being completely mapped and studied, and man's knowledge of it is only partial.

That is not to say that man is unfamiliar with the sea. Men have ventured on the ocean for centuries, using it as both an avenue of exploration and a means of communication and trade. Early sailors sailed the inland seas, especially the Mediterranean. They were followed by Leif Ericson and Christopher Columbus, both of whom crossed the North Atlantic to reach America. Perhaps even earlier than that, Polynesians of the southwest and central Pacific sailed eastward to the coast of South America, using only the prevailing winds and primitive navigational aids to get them across the thousands of miles of open ocean. To these early sailors the sea was a featureless broad expanse of wave-driven water.

Variously gray, green, blue, or black, the sea's color depends on the sky above it, on microscopic creatures that inhabit its upper layers, and on the material of the bottom beneath it (coral reefs, mud, sand, and so on). Seldom, however, does the ocean's surface reveal much about its depths. In a few places, of course, where the water is unusually calm and there is no bottom turbulence, it is possible to look down several hundred feet and see undersea plants, fish, and rocks, but such conditions are unusual. Over most of its surface, the sea is an unrevealing blank.

Divers who explore the sea also seldom learn much about the bottom. This is partly because light can penetrate only a short distance into the ocean. Although both the visible and the invisible portions of the electromagnetic spectrum pass through the atmosphere, little of the spectrum reaches very far into the sea—perhaps a thousand feet, under the most favorable circumstances.

A diver, sinking through the water, sees it turn first green, then blue or violet, and finally inky black, a darkness deeper and more concealing than any night on any continent. The darkness at the bottom of the sea is so all-enveloping that the few men who have been exposed to it say it is impossible to describe, that it must be experienced to be understood.

The darkness is eternal. Except for the occasional "fire-flies," the light organs found on the bodies of many deep-sea fish, there is nothing to breach the blackness.

Darkness, however, is only one of the barriers to direct examination of the sea floor. A towering column of water at least two miles in height stands above the typical bottom with pressures of thousands of pounds for each square inch of surface area. Only the strongest of steel walls can keep a man from being crushed to death at such pressures. Because men must breathe air that is at or near the pressure at sea level, a human body deep in the sea would be squeezed into a tiny balloon by the immense weight of the water around it. Fish, which extract oxygen from the water through their gills, are able to live at the bottom because the pressure inside their bodies remains approximately equal to that of the ocean around them. But just as men cannot survive at the sea bottom, so deep-sea fish pop outward like balloons when they are suddenly brought to the surface. At sea level the pressure inside their bodies is far greater than that outside.

Pressure, darkness, and the lack of a sea-level atmos-phere—all these and more restrict man's ability to work on or look directly at the bottom of the ocean. Instead, he has been forced to rely on indirect methods of examining the sea floor. Such methods have not come easily. Although men have sailed the seas for centuries, until recently their voyages have been made in ignorance of the ocean bottom. Ignorance made the deep sea a fearsome place to early sailors. Their imaginations peopled it with monsters, mythical gods, and other terrors.

Man's interest in the sea floor, however, developed not because he wished to destroy the figures of his imagination with facts, but for a more practical reason. Sailors plying the coasts of Europe in the early days of sail discovered that rocks, shoals, and sandbars tore out the bottoms of their vessels or left them aground. If men were to avoid such perils, they must locate and map them.

First, however, the sailors had to discover ways to pinpoint their position on the ocean accurately. On land man could use permanent landmarks to tell where he was, but the sea was a blank. Man had to learn to fix his position on the sea's surface by navigation.

Navigation depends on the use of mathematics. The sun or fixed stars must be sighted; the angle of the sighting must be measured; the drift and the distance covered from the last sighting and similar factors must be estimated.

Not until the compass and the sextant were invented did sailors have the ability to locate and chart underwater features of the ocean bottoms accurately.

The problem then became one of finding the obstacles themselves. Since they were seldom seen, they had to be sought out indirectly. To accomplish this, sailors began to use sounding lines, lengths of light rope weighted at one end. The weighted end of the rope was tossed over the side and allowed to fall through the water until it reached bottom. A measurement of the amount of line required to reach the ocean floor gave the approximate depth of water beneath a ship.

When ships moved close to shore, their captains stationed

linesmen in the bows to make continuous soundings. The call of the linesmen told of shoaling water. Sometimes, too, linesmen stuck a lump of tallow or wax to the bottom of the lead that weighted their lines. With it, they could recover sand, mud, or gravel and get an indication of the kind of bottom over which the ship was passing. A bottom with a lot of sand and gravel might be expected to have fewer large, sharp rocks than one where no sand or gravel could be recovered.

Most soundings were made near shore in shallow water. Not until the nineteenth century did sailors consider sounding in deeper waters. Again, this came about partly because of a practical need to know. Submarine cables were being perfected and laid from one continent to another to allow telephone and telegraph communication. To lay such lines, men had to know something about the ocean depths.

The nineteenth century also saw a general awakening of interest in all branches of science, and the desire to explore the sea bottom simply because it was unknown territory also had much to do with touching bottom in the Atlantic. The first attempt at deep-sea exploration there was on January 3, 1840, when an Englishman, James Clark Ross, unreeled 14,550 feet of hemp line before he finally managed to reach the bottom. As scientists now know, this is not far from the average depth in all the oceans of the world.

As time went on, other deep-sea soundings were made, especially in the most traveled of seas, the Atlantic, but little was done to evaluate the information thus gained until 1854. Then Matthew F. Maury of the United States Navy began to assemble soundings from many different sources to create a *bathometric chart* of the floor of the Atlantic.

Maury carefully plotted known depths from soundings on a map. Equal depths on the map then were joined by lines, somewhat as children join the dots in a dot-and-line drawing to make a picture. The result was a series of *contours,* not unlike the contour lines that make up a topographic map of land surfaces.

The difference between Maury's charts and those of land surveyors was in what they measured. Topographic maps show elevations above sea level. Bathometric charts show depths below sea level. Both give an approximate picture of differences in depth or elevation, as if one were looking down on the land or on the bottom of the sea emptied of water.

Maury's pioneering work in assessing the deep-sea bottom was only one of many contributions he made to the science of oceanography. He also founded what was to become the United States Coast and Geodetic Survey and wrote guidebooks for ocean navigation.

Most of Maury's work was done in the Atlantic. The Pacific, the largest of the world's oceans, remained little explored and some other seas, the Arctic and Antarctic, for example, were still blanks on world bathometric charts in the nineteenth century. Clearly, a more general survey of the world's oceans was needed.

To begin this task, the Royal Society of England, then one of the most august scientific bodies in the world, decided to commission a worldwide oceanographic expedition. Under the direction of C. Wyville Thomson, professor of natural history at the University of Edinburgh, the society chartered H.M.S. *Challenger* and fitted it with tanks, hauls, nets, dredges, microscopes, thermometers, and other equip-

ment. The ship was staffed by six scientists especially selected for their knowledge and interest in the sea.

The *Challenger* set sail from England in December,
1872. For most of the next year it took up stations in the
Atlantic; that is, it stood still upon the surface of the sea
and made observations. The *Challenger* crossed from one
side of the Atlantic to the other. Then, late in 1873, it
sailed south into the Antarctic Ocean, eventually reaching
a point fourteen hundred miles from the South Pole. Later
it moved into the Pacific for a series of new stations, slowly
working its way westward. Off the Marianas Islands it
sounded to a depth of 26,850 feet in a part of the sea that
has since come to be known as the Challenger Deep. The
Challenger Deep is still believed to be the deepest part in
any ocean. (In 1957, during the International Geophysical
Year, a Russian research vessel, the *Vityaz,* sounded to a
depth of 36,198 feet near the same point.)

After its Pacific Ocean survey, the *Challenger* continued
on its way around the world through the Indian Ocean.
On May 24, 1876, after having spent three and a half years
circumnavigating the globe and having observed at 362
stations, the *Challenger* finally returned to England. The expedition had visited every major ocean of the world except
the Arctic and had charted millions of miles of ocean,
sounding the bottom, gathering specimens of sea life—
many of them unknown until then—and collecting an immense amount of information.

No other single voyage of discovery in man's history
provided him with so much new knowledge. So much information had been gathered by members of the *Challenger*
expedition that it took twenty-three years for them to com-

pile the more than fifty volumes of reports that constitute its story. Except for the International Geophysical Year, 1957–1958, man has never mounted so thorough a scientific assault on the planet on which he lives.

The *Challenger* voyage gave new impetus to oceanography and marine geology, the two disciplines of science concerned with the sea and the sea bottom. The voyage also proved the value of specially equipped oceanographic vessels and their ability to gather large amounts of information directly at sea. Largely as a result of the *Challenger* expedition, scientists in many different parts of the world began establishing oceanographic study centers. In the United States the three best-known institutions are Scripps Institution of Oceanography in California, Woods Hole Oceanographic Institution in Massachusetts, and the Lamont-Doherty Geological Observatory in New York.

It would be incorrect to assume, however, that a great amount of work immediately followed the success of the *Challenger*'s voyage. The United States did not officially commission an oceanographic vessel of its own until 1882, when the U.S.S. *Albatross,* a two-hundred-foot, one-thousand-ton ship, was specially constructed for this purpose. Under the direction of Alexander Agassiz, a member of a famous scientific family, the *Albatross* explored large areas of the Pacific and Indian oceans and the Caribbean Sea.

Several western European nations commissioned similar craft during the last years of the nineteenth century and the years before World War I. Most used the methods pioneered by the *Challenger,* although soundings continued to be made generally by dropping lines over the side.

Agassiz was the first to substitute steel wire, then more readily available, for hemp rope.

World War I brought a major new development in exploring the ocean floor, *echo sounding.* Echo sounding, also known as *sonar,* was developed because of the introduction of submarine warfare into that conflict. The ability of submarines to move about beneath the surface of the ocean for long periods of time made them difficult to see and almost impossible to attack. To locate them, wartime scientists devised echo sounding.

Echo sounding depends on the ability of water, like air, to carry sound waves. If a *ping* of sound is emitted from a sonar transmitter, it moves through the water until it strikes something solid. The wave is then reflected back to a receiver on the same ship that sent the original signal. By knowing the speed at which sound will pass through salt water, scientists can use sonar to estimate the range, or distance, of an object they have detected. Direction can also be determined.

During World War I surface ships used sonar to detect and attack submarines. Submarines also occasionally reversed the process and used echo sounding to detect targets for their torpedoes. Echo sounding became a kind of underwater eye for both friend and foe. After the war it was used to find the distance from a ship to the ocean bottom. A ping of sound directed from a vessel downward, if sufficiently powerful, could reach the bottom and be reflected upward to the sonar receiver. Just as it was used to measure the distance from a surface vessel to an enemy submarine, so could it be used as a substitute for the more cumbersome sounding line.

Echo sounding had another advantage. Properly connected to a moving paper tape, it could provide an almost continuous record of the bottom. This, in effect, was a profile of the rises and falls in the sea floor directly beneath the vessel carrying the equipment. If the ship sailed in a straight line for a long distance, the track it covered, properly matched with map location, gave an exact picture of the undersea features. It was as if scientists had been able to slice through the ocean and the earth beneath it with a giant knife, much like cutting through a piece of cake and exposing its layers.

Although an accurate, continuous representation of the bottom of the sea will appear on a sonar recorder, echo sounding is not as simple and easy as this description would indicate. Many things can interfere with sonar signals: schools of fish, variations in water density, temperature differences, and the strength of the sonar signal itself. Some echo sounders are not strong enough to penetrate to the bottom in the very deep sea. Nor is it possible to maintain a completely continuous record of the bottom. Between each ping of sound emitted by a transmitter and its return as an echo to the sonar receiver, the ship sending it passes over a small portion of the sea floor. That area is not covered by the sound wave and goes unrecorded. Generally, however, this is so small a part of the bottom that it is unimportant. Echo sounding is still far faster and easier than sounding with a weighted line, and its use after World War I opened vast new areas of the ocean floor to exploration and mapping.

Most of this exploration took place in the Atlantic. With the beginning of World War II, however, the United States found itself involved in a major war at sea in the Pacific, the largest of the world's oceans, and not much traveled and charted. Before World War II large stretches of the Pacific's bottom had never been sounded, but now an increasing number of warships were fitted with echo-sounding recorders. The result was a sudden expansion of knowledge about this sea and an increased interest in its floor.

The Pacific has many unique features besides its size. It is circled by the greatest chain of earthquake fault lines in the world, and around its basin in a "circle of fire" are most of the earth's active volcanoes. It contains the deepest underwater trenches on earth, many of them located at the eastern edge of island arcs in the western Pacific (the area around Japan and China) and it has several deep-bottom topographic features that seem unique. The puzzle of all this and the question of why the Pacific is so large are matters that have come to intrigue those who study the sea floor and will be discussed at more length in Chapter 2 of this book.

The wartime exploration of the Pacific floor also included one of the greatest single echo-sounding expeditions in man's history. It happened because of Harry Hess, a marine geologist then serving as a reserve naval officer aboard the U.S.S. *Cape Johnson*. Hess had been assigned to the *Cape Johnson* as it was being outfitted and had managed to have it equipped with a very powerful echo sounder. With it, he accumulated valuable records of the bottom while the ship sailed around the Pacific. As the war came to a close, the *Cape Johnson* was part of a fleet of many ships sailing north from the South Pacific to Japan. Hess persuaded the fleet's commander to order that all ships under his command be equipped with echo-sounding gear to record bottom profiles continuously during this voyage. The result was a great swath of exploration of the sea bottom two thousand miles long, stretching across much of the western Pacific.

The interest in undersea exploration begun during World War II has continued. The Office of Naval Research, greatly expanded by the war, now funds studies in all parts of the world—and in space as well. Much of the work of undersea exploration in the Pacific has been carried on by a fleet of oceanographic vessels from Scripps Institution. Lamont-Doherty and Woods Hole have undertaken additional voyages in the Atlantic and Indian oceans. The Antarctic has become a permanent base for land and sea exploration under an international treaty. Even the floor of the Arctic Ocean, for so long hidden beneath a layer of ice, has been studied, both from ice islands on the surface of that sea and through the use of nuclear-powered submarines, which have traversed it from side to side without having to surface.

Efforts at studying the ocean bottom have been extended far beyond sounding. Geologists have discovered it is not enough to know what the bottom looks like in profile. They have also sought to study it directly.

The most obvious way to see the bottom of the ocean is to dive down and look at it. The first successful effort at direct observation of the bottom of the sea was made in the 1930's by William Beebe. Beebe, aware that conventional diving gear was inadequate for the pressures of the deep sea, constructed a special diving vehicle, which he called a *bathysphere*.

Beebe's bathysphere was a large, round steel ball whose

walls were thick enough to withstand the enormous pressures exerted by water on the ocean floor. In the wall of the ball, he installed a thick quartz window. Electric lights, powered by a cable attached to the lines that lowered the bathysphere into the sea, provided illumination. Oxygen for Beebe and his assistant to breathe was carried in tanks. The bathysphere had no power of its own and could not move about once it reached the bottom, but it did offer mankind his first direct look at the lower depths of the sea.

On August 15, 1934, Beebe and his associate, Otis Barton, were sealed in the bathysphere and lowered 3,028 feet to the bottom of the Caribbean Sea. This record went unchallenged until 1949, when Barton reached a depth of 4,050 feet off the coast of California.

Beebe's bathysphere was the first of a series of deep-sea diving devices, the best known of which is the *Trieste,* which was called a bathyscaphe and was developed in the 1950's by two Swiss scientists, Auguste Piccard and his son Jacques. Earlier Auguste Piccard and his brother Jean Félix had made pioneer high-altitude balloon ascents, and the Piccards' bathyscaphe was a reverse version of balloon ascension. Instead of ascending, the *Trieste* was built to descend freely into the ocean.

The *Trieste*'s "balloon" was several tanks of gasoline contained in a hull similar to that of a small ship. Because gasoline is slightly lighter than water, it allowed the *Trieste* to float on the surface of the sea. Suspended beneath the *Trieste* was a steel ball similar to Beebe's original bathysphere. The craft descended because of steel balls, stored in bins on the bottom of the *Trieste* and held in place by electromagnets. Their weight was greater than the flotation offered by the gasoline in the tanks. So long as the magnets were operating, the balls clung to them. When the current was turned off, the balls fell to the bottom of the sea, and the *Trieste* rose to the surface like a balloon. Two small propellers powered by electric engines gave the *Trieste* limited horizontal and vertical movement.

After the *Trieste*'s ability had been demonstrated by dives in the sea around Europe, it was purchased by the United States Navy and taken to the western Pacific. There, in 1960, it carried Jacques Piccard and Lieutenant Don Walsh, a Navy officer, 35,800 feet down to the bottom of the Challenger Deep, the deepest man has ever gone in any ocean. Later, refitted and moved to the Atlantic, the *Trieste* helped locate the wreckage of the nuclear submarine *Thresher* after it had been lost at sea during a practice dive.

The *Trieste* was the first of many maneuverable deep-sea diving vehicles—among them the *Aluminaut, Alvin, Deepstar,* and *Deepquest*—that have since explored the deep sea and provided a few men with a direct look at the bottom.

For the most part, man's view of the sea floor has not been a particularly exciting one. The bottom revealed by such dives usually is a soft mud, or ooze. No plants grow at the bottom of the sea, because no sunlight can penetrate to such depths. The fish, starfish, worms, and other creatures that dwell at the bottom are few in number and are seldom spectacular in appearance. They survive by living off one another in a series of interlocking food chains similar to those found at or above the sea's surface. Quite a few deep-sea fish carry their own illumination with them as they swim about in the inky blackness, mostly to recognize their own species so they can find mates and stay together in groups.

Wind does not blow across the bottom of the sea, nor

does ice form there. Although currents of water sometimes sweep the deep ocean floor, little is known about them or about how they affect change. There is no cracking and breaking of rocks because of extreme differences in temperature, as there is on the surface of the continents; the wind does not erode the sea's long plains; no rivers grind down boulders into sand.

The bottom of the sea is much less subject to change than are the faces of the continents. Yet it would be wrong to believe that the sea bottom never changes. In places there are sudden and swift movements of water called *turbidity currents*. Often, especially in the Pacific, undersea

This picture, magnified 100 times, shows skeletons of various forms of Radiolaria in sediment cores taken in the Caroline Ridge area of the western Pacific Ocean. In life, these tiny organisms lived near the ocean surface, and upon death their skeletons fell to the seabed to become entombed in the sediments. By carefully studying them, scientists can determine how long ago they lived and can learn much about the history of the ocean.

Courtesy Scripps Institution of Oceanography

earthquakes cause abrupt shifts up or down in the level of the floor. Finally, the bottom of the sea is the depository for everything—on the surface of the continents as well as in the ocean itself. It is a great graveyard, the final resting place for many sea creatures and for materials washed from the land by water into the sea. This debris makes up *deep-sea sediments,* chronicles of the past "written" in chronological order from the bottom layer to the top layer of the ocean floor.

The story of deep-sea sediments is central to man's desire to probe and plumb the deep ocean, for the layering of sediments, no matter what their source, is a record without parallel on the land surface of the earth. Whereas the continents have been uplifted and dropped, crushed, eroded, and jumbled by changes in the earth's crust and by the forces of the atmosphere, large parts of the sea bottom seem to have been left undisturbed for thousands, even millions of years. Properly interpreted, they can tell much about the time before man's recorded history.

Sediments come from two principal sources. Some are the finely ground products of land erosion washed down rivers and shorelines and turned into gravel, sand, and mud. They fan out at the mouths of streams and are laid down there or in shallow bays or inlets along the seacoast. Then they gradually move farther and farther out to sea, eventually to be deposited at the bottom of the deep ocean.

The minute skeletons of microscopic sea creatures make up an equally important part of the sediments on the sea floor. Many of these skeletons come from a species of creature called *Foraminifera,* but two other types, *radiolarians* and *diatoms,* are also found on the bottom of the ocean. These animals are so small that many thousands of them can live in a cubic foot of water. As they grow, they use lime from seawater to form a bony shell about themselves. In time they either die or shed their shell. The empty shells drift downward through ever darkening water to the ocean bottom. As they do, the seawater dissolves the lime, leaving only the thin silica skeletons.

By the billions and trillions these remnants of once living creatures settle to the bottom of the ocean. However, this deposition of death is not uniform throughout the world. Some parts of the sea floor seem to consist merely of mud and nonorganic ooze. Elsewhere, in the northern Pacific, for example, beds of the deep-sea skeletal remains are found that are hundreds, sometimes thousands, of feet in depth. From such beds scientists can gain clues about what was happening on the earth during the time when the creatures died. It is also possible to match the skeletons with epochs of geologic time on the continental surface. The examination, measurement, and interpretation of deep-sea sediments thus is of great importance in marine geology and in geology in general.

In the past, one of the problems in studying sediments has been the difficulty of lifting them from the bottom of the ocean to its surface. Like any story, the book of sediments has a beginning, a middle, and an end. The beginning of its chronicles lies in the deepest depth beneath the sea. Since sediments are deposited from above, the earliest layers were put down first, the most recent last. The layers have been deposited horizontally, yet they must be read vertically. The layers must be cut through from top to bottom and removed in order.

It is, of course, possible to dredge the sea bottom and haul samples of sediments to the top, but this has the great disadvantage of disturbing and mixing the information the sediments contain, often making their message hopelessly confusing. Dredges are being used to raise parts of the ocean bottom to the surface, but they are of little value in the study of sediments. Just as this book would be almost meaningless if its pages were not arranged in numerical order, so sedimentary samples are of little value if they are not in proper chronologic order.

Knowing this, in 1935, C. S. Piggot, an oceanographer, devised a way to gather sediments without disturbing their order. His device is called a *corer,* or a *tube corer,* and it operates on the same principle as the kitchen tool used to core apples. An apple corer is a round tube sharpened at one end. It can be pressed into an apple to surround and remove the core. An oceanographic corer does the same thing, except that it is plunged into the bottom of the ocean to remove a representative sample of the bottom and bring it intact to the sea's surface.

The simplest coring device is a steel pipe about an inch in diameter to which a heavy weight is attached. The lower end of the pipe is open, but is covered with a piece of plastic when it is dropped into the sea. The pipe and weight are slid down an anchored line to the ocean bottom. There the weight thrusts the open end of the pipe into the sea floor, breaking the seal and allowing samples of layers to be caught inside the pipe. Steel spring fingers attached to the open end of the pipe then emerge to prevent the sample from dropping back into the water. The corer is hauled to the surface, and its sample is extruded by a steel rod, which is pushed against the sample until it emerges onto a tray for examination.

To reach greater depths or to penetrate consolidated sediments a more powerful device invented by the Swedish oceanographer Börje Kullenberg is used. The Kullenberg corer is thirty feet long, larger by two inches in diameter than the Piggot corer, and is equipped at its upper end with a piston that can drive almost the entire length of the corer into the sea bottom. Otherwise, it is operated in much the same way as the Piggot corer.

Coring offers a way to sample the composition and layering of the deep sea floor without actually traveling to it in person. The core samples gathered by coring devices lowered to the bottom have come from many different places in various parts of the ocean. They tell much about the past of the sea and something about what happened on the surface of the continents. They also give some hints about what may be coming in the future. They do not, however, tell much about what lies below the uppermost part of the sea floor.

Marine geologists are not positive about how the bottom of the sea is constructed and what lies between the bottom of the sea and the earth's mantle, but they believe sediments are an important part of the formation of the deep-sea floor. As layer after layer of material is deposited from above, the weight of seawater on top of the material must squeeze it and push it more and more closely together until it becomes similar to rock, or as geologists say, becomes *consolidated*. Consolidated material may eventually be driven into the mantle itself.

The deeper layers of the crust are of great interest to

geologists, but for a long time these layers have been difficult to study. Most efforts have been indirect. One way has been through the use of *seismic waves.* Seismic sounding is, in some ways, similar to echo sounding. It rests on the ability of the rocks and sediments of the earth's crust to transmit waves of energy.

Geologists have known for more than a century that the earth transmits energetic waves, because of their studies of volcanoes and earthquakes. Earthquakes, in particular, happen when there is a buildup of pressure along a fault in the earth's crust. When the fault, driven by pressure, slips horizontally, vertically, or in both directions, the pent-up energy that has forced the two sides of the fault together is transmitted in all directions through the earth. In very large earthquakes the amount of energy released is great. It may pass completely through the earth. In less severe earthquakes this may not happen, but in any earthquake some energy is released into the rock and soil of the earth's crust, mantle, and core.

By using this knowledge and making careful measurements of the speed at which seismic waves travel through different underground formations, petroleum geologists devised a way to explore for oil on land. They set off small explosions, usually using dynamite dropped down a hole. When the dynamite exploded at one point, the time of the explosion was radioed or telephoned to a second point some distance away. Measurements of the arrival time of seismic waves and their patterns were recorded at the second station. With such exploration it often was possible to find underground formations called *salt domes,* where pools of oil may be located.

Seismic exploration of the deep-sea floor follows a similar procedure. Marine geologists, however, do not attempt to drill holes in the bottom of the ocean in which to set their explosive charges. Instead, they drop depth charges over the side of a vessel and explode them underwater. A second ship trailing *hydrophones,* special underwater listening devices, waits a measured distance away. The first ship signals to the second when an explosion has been detonated. The second then records the arrival of waves at its hydrophones.

The seismic waves generated by the depth charges pass through both water and the bottom of the sea. In fact, they pass more rapidly through the solid material of the bottom than they do through water. Some waves, of course, will travel only through water to reach the hydrophones. Others will travel through both water and the bottom material. Some waves will be reflected by the bottom and bounce back into the water. Others will be refracted; that is, they will enter the sea floor, be deflected through it for a time, and then emerge once more into seawater to be detected by the hydrophones.

Matching seismic sea patterns with patterns gathered on the continental surface gives marine geologists an idea of the thickness and composition of the bottom of the sea. From many such measurements geologists have concluded that the crust of the earth beneath the oceans is much thinner than that part of the crust known as the continents. The continental crust may be thirty to fifty miles thick where there are large continental mountain ranges such as the Rockies or the Himalayas, but most of the crust beneath the sea is only three to six miles deep. The reason for this difference is not yet understood, but geologists generally attribute it to *isostasy,* the balancing of one part of the crust with another. Because the continents are thicker, they must be balanced by the weight of the ocean's waters. This makes possible a much thinner crustal surface beneath the seas than through the continents.

The thinness of the crust under the ocean makes it a tantalizing area of exploration for marine geologists. They know that just beneath it lies the earth's mantle, which surrounds the core itself. The materials in the mantle are as much a mystery as the reasons for its apparent semifluid state, but clearly it has important effects on the crust—and on us.

The crust beneath the oceans is so thin, in fact, that for many years schemes have been suggested to drill through it to reach the mantle. These proposals finally culminated in the voyages of the *Glomar Challenger.*

Chapter 2

THE SHAPE
OF THE BOTTOM

The earth, as man has been aware for several centuries, is a giant ball spinning in space around the sun. Actually, it is *oblate* rather than perfectly round—that is, slightly thicker at its middle than at its poles—but for most purposes, including those of this book, it can be considered a sphere. It is also, as most schoolchildren quickly learn, approximately eight thousand miles in diameter and about twenty-five thousand miles in circumference.

After these facts, however, man's familiarity with his world is limited. This is because most of man's experience with the earth has been with its crust. It is on the crust of the earth that he lives—or to be more precise, in the *biosphere,* the thin envelope of gases and water that makes up the oceans and the atmosphere and coats the crust like a film.

Man is able to move over the earth's surface through this coating for long distances, but he seldom travels more than a mile or two above or below sea level. Because man has such lateral freedom, he tends to forget the severe limitations of the biosphere. On one side of it lies the emptiness of deep space. On the other is the unknown of the earth's deeper layers. Man knows what is beyond the upper depths of the crust only through inference and indirect measurement. From such studies he has concluded that the earth's interior can be divided into four general areas: the *crust,* the *mantle,* and the *inner* and *outer cores.*

Man knows something about the crust. He even has an approximate idea of its thickness. The downward limit of the crust, the division between crust and mantle, was discovered in 1909 by a Yugoslav geologist, Andrija Mohorovičić, as he was measuring the seismic waves of energy generated by an earthquake. Mohorovičić's measurements turned up a difference in the speed with which waves were recorded at two different *seismographs,* devices used to measure the intensity of earthquakes.

By carefully analyzing his data, Mohorovičić was able to show that the different speeds at which the waves traveled were caused by a difference in the material through which they passed. The waves traveling through the lighter material near the top of the crust moved at a speed different from those that passed through the heavier material beneath it.

The lighter material—which makes up the continental portion of the crust—has since come to be called *sial* because it is a combination of the elements *silicon* and *aluminum.* The heavier portion of the crust is called *sima* because

it is composed of *silicon* and *magnesium*. The level at which
the crust separates from the mantle beneath it is called the
Mohorovičić discontinuity, or often, more simply, the *Moho
discontinuity.*

Below the Moho is the mantle, a region whose lower limit
is not known with certainty, but which is believed to be
about eighteen hundred miles from the earth's surface. The
mantle's composition is unknown, but geologists generally
assume it to be thick and viscous, somewhat like very heavy,
thick plastic. Our only hint of its composition is from volcanic eruptions, which may be made of mantle material.

Beneath the mantle lie the earth's inner and outer cores.
They are heavy, perhaps mostly nickel and iron. The outer
core may be solid, but the inner heart of the earth is prob-

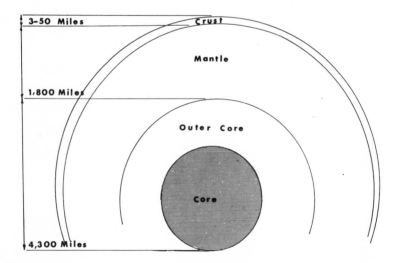

The relative relation of the various segments of the earth's interior. Drawing is not to scale.

ably molten, kept in this state by the great heat and pressure at the center of the planet. The passage of seismic waves through the earth is what makes geologists think the earth's inner core is liquid metal. Some waves generated by earthquakes will not pass through liquids, but are absorbed by them. Hence when these waves do not pass through the earth's inner core, but are absorbed by it, they must indicate that the core is a liquid.

The earth's crust is rigid and brittle. It moves along well-established cracks, or *faults*. Faults are the focus of earth tremors. The movement of opposing sides of a fault is what causes the earth to move and quake. Usually, earth tremors move sections of the crust along a fault only an inch or two at a time, but in very great earthquakes, such as the one that almost destroyed San Francisco in 1906, the earth can slip many feet.

Movement along a fault line may be horizontal, vertical, or in both directions at the same time. The waves of energy released by an earthquake are used to locate the point in the crust where it happened, its *focus*. Earthquakes occur at depths beneath the surface that vary from a few to several hundred miles. The focus of an earthquake, plus the point on the earth's surface where the quake is felt, its *epicenter,* help to tell where earth faults are.

By measuring many different earthquakes with many different foci and epicenters, geologists have charted and mapped most of the major land faults in the world. Some, such as the San Andreas Fault in California—the location of the 1906 earthquake—have been studied over their entire length, often almost foot by foot. Others, especially those beneath the sea, are less well known, and occasionally faults long dormant or previously unknown wake to life again.

Faults and earthquakes also help geologists gain insight into the deep layers of the planet beyond their direct visual examination. Earthquakes generate three different kinds of waves. P (primary) waves, S (secondary, or shear) waves, and low-intensity surface waves called by several different names.

P and S waves travel completely through the earth if generated by large-enough earthquakes, although S waves may be absorbed by the earth's core. Surface waves travel shorter distances just below the surface of the crust.

The discovery of seismic waves and their relationship to material in the crust has been of great importance in understanding the bottom of the sea. The waves serve as indirect measuring devices to "see" the depth and composition of lower layers of the earth's crust, including that part beneath the oceans.

Volcanoes are another natural phenomenon that helps us to understand the earth. Volcanoes are holes, or *conduits,* in the crust through which very hot material deep in the earth rises to the surface. When contained in the earth, this material is called *magma.* After it has been erupted by a volcano and has spilled on the earth's surface, this same material is called either *lava,* or *ejecta.* Some magma may be formed in the crust itself, but geologists generally believe that most of it comes from the mantle, squeezed to the surface by pressure and heat.

Few volcanic eruptions are predictable, and not all volcanoes erupt the same kinds of material. The way in which volcanoes erupt and what they eject allows earth scientists to classify them into groups. *Shield volcanoes* erupt a thin lava repeatedly over millions of years, building up their bulk through successive outpourings of lava. *Lava dome* volcanoes erupt a very thick lava (basaltic), often with enormous explosive force. *Stratovolcanoes* erupt successive layers of ash and cinder and flows of lava, and reach great heights by piling layer on layer. *Cinder cones* release ejecta that consists mostly of fine cinders and ash.

Volcanoes tend to be located near one another in chains or belts. The largest number ring the Pacific Ocean basin in what has been called the circle of fire. This great ring of volcanoes stretches down the coast of North and South America, runs through the south and southwestern Pacific up along the island chains of the western Pacific to the Kurile and Aleutian islands, and finally rejoins the North American continent.

Another major belt of volcanoes runs through the Mediterranean Sea and the borders of Africa and Asia.

Volcanoes can be found also beneath the surface of the sea and occasionally rise from it. One of the newest of these volcanic islands is Surtsey, which suddenly appeared in the Atlantic Ocean south of Iceland in 1965. Surtsey is one of an irregularly spaced chain of fiery islands that begins in Iceland and includes the Azores, Ascension and Tristan da Cunha islands, and Saint Paul's Rocks.

The volcanic islands of the Atlantic are located atop a high ridge of undersea mountains, which follows the same general north-south direction through the middle of that ocean. This mountain range, indented along its top, is called the *Mid-Atlantic Ridge*. It is part of a worldwide series of ridges and rises, which branch east and west from the South

Atlantic into both the Pacific and Indian oceans. Were the oceans not in place, this series of ridges would give the surface of the earth the appearance of a baseball with spiraling seams running around its circumference.

Other undersea mountains, both mountain chains and isolated peaks, exist elsewhere at the bottom. Some are similar to mountains on land, but others are strange, flat-topped formations called *guyots* after a Swiss-born American oceanographer, Arnold Guyot. Between these two variations in undersea peaks are long, flat stretches of featureless ocean bottom called *abysmal plains*.

Ridges and rises are not the only features of the ocean bottom. Deep trenches can be found in the South Pacific close to the west coast of South America and along the island chains of the western Pacific and Alaska. Long, narrow, and steep, they often extend thousands of feet below the floor around them. Many are V-shaped, but others have a U configuration. Many also lie close to the foci of undersea earthquakes.

In the eastern Pacific off the coast of North and South America is another strange set of features: long, straight, narrow, shallow drops in the ocean floor called *fracture zones*. Several hundred miles apart, they may run east and west for thousands of miles. Recently, similar features have been found in other ocean floors.

What do all these features mean? What is their relationship to one another?

Geologists have puzzled over these questions for years. Gradually it has become clear to them that most ocean features must have some relationship to even larger features of the earth's crust, features that are related not only to what can be seen on the earth's surface or detected beneath the seas, but also to conditions in the deep interior of the earth.

Scientists have begun to see that the earth's surface is divided into great sections, or *plates,* which are constantly moving. Apparently, as these plates grind together or pull apart, volcanoes, earth faults and earthquakes, deep ocean trenches, and other crustal features are created. The plates have been called *tectonic plates,* and the theory that explains them is the *plate tectonic theory. Tectonic* is a Greek word that means "builder" or "carpenter." Its use in this context is intended to show that such forces are at work in shaping the crust.

At least ten major tectonic plates and several minor ones now have been defined by scientists. They include the American, Pacific, African, Eurasian, Somali, Indo-Australian, Philippine, Nazca, Antarctic, Caribbean, and Cocos. Each of these names indicates the location of the plate on the earth's surface. Thus the American plate includes North and South America and a portion of the Atlantic Ocean. The Cocos plate is named for the area around Cocos Island off the coast of Costa Rica, and the Somali plate refers to Somalia, an area on the northeast coast of Africa.

What moves the plates?

Geologists are not sure. They are, of course, unable to see beneath the crust into the mantle and core of the earth. Moreover, plate movement is very slow, measured in man's time. It takes place over millions of years. Yet a theory explaining what may cause the plates to shift has been proposed. One of its premises is that the earth is a giant heat engine. Most of this heat is stored in the earth's core,

The major plates of the world's crust, outlined by the earth's system of ridges, rises, trenches, and earthquake faults. Minor plates are not shown.

in its molten heart. All heat flows from hot material to cooler material; in this case the heat flows from the center of the earth outward through the mantle to the crust. As the heat is conveyed outward the process seems to include the movement of portions of the mantle, although the exact nature of the process is not known. The mantle's plastic material must be driven by the core's heat, rising slowly from the depths of the earth toward the crust in great currents.

You can see some of the way this may happen by boiling a pot of water or soup on the stove. Heat from the stove burner touches the bottom of the pan. The pan's heat, in turn, heats the lower level of the liquid, forcing it upward to the surface. Once the heated liquid from the bottom reaches the top of the pot, it is cooled by its contact with air. Cooling takes place as the heat is transferred from the molecules of the water to the molecules of the air. Once cooled, the liquid sinks back toward the heat at the bottom of the pot, and once again it is moved to the surface. A cycle is set up in which the liquid moves from bottom to top, from top to bottom, in continuous currents. So long as heat is added to the soup and the soup is cooled, the cycling action will continue.

Scientists call this kind of thermal motion *convection,* and the current that is set up is a *convection current.* The same kind of convection currents may exist in the earth's mantle. In fact, many geologists believe there are several such currents, moving in separate circles, or *convection cells,* within the mantle. The mantle's convection cells are much larger than those of the soup, of course, and cover hundreds of thousands of miles, but the currents in these cells are moved by the same kind of energy, heat, that generates in a pot of soup. Instead of taking only a few seconds, as happens in the pot, a complete cycle in the mantle's convection cells may take thousands of years. What is important, however, is not the length of time this cycle takes, but the effect that the transfer of heat from the mantle to the bottom of the crust has on the earth's surface.

The points of pressure created by convection cells on the crust may mark the borders of tectonic plates. As pressure on the underside of the crust increases, it may cause the rigid, brittle crust to crack and move. But this is not the only effect. The material in the convection cell's current must cool and move back again through the mantle, to be reheated by the core, and its flow downward may also affect the crust. This downthrusting current may actually pull at the bottom of the crust and drag it along, downward, at an angle. When this happens, submarine trenches may be created. Perhaps in them the earth's crust is being sucked inward into the mantle.

The downthrusting of convection-cell currents may cause large puckers, or wrinkles, in the crust as well. Such surface effects are most evident in the island chains of the western Pacific. Deep trenches, among them the deepest in the world, lie along the edges of the Philippines, Japan, and other island arcs. It is as if the dropping of the crust is caus- ing the magma to be pushed up beyond the trenches. Not only do the island arcs of the western Pacific contain many volcanoes, many of them are also the focus of earthquakes.

While all this conveniently fits the theory of tectonic plate formation and movement, what of the other ocean features? Not all islands fit the arc pattern. The most ob- vious exception in the Pacific is the Hawaiian Islands. They lie in the center of that ocean, are rarely visited by earth- quakes, are isolated from other surface features, and do not have any trenches about them. At first glance they seem unrelated to either plate movement or convection cells. The same is true, at first glance, of the islands of the Atlantic. The Atlantic has no island chains. Its islands, too, are iso- lated single surface features, separated from one another by long distances of open sea.

But the Hawaiian Islands and the islands of the Atlantic have a common characteristic. They are all volcanic in origin. In fact, the islands of Hawaii are individual shield volcanoes, which have heaped up immense piles of lava over millions of years, creating huge mountains that rise from the depths of the Pacific to as much as thirteen thousand feet above the ocean surface.

The Atlantic islands are volcanoes too, but of a different kind. They erupt periodically, but less frequently than the active conduits of Hawaii.

A further look at Hawaii shows that it is also a part of a chain of undersea mountains that begins in the far northwestern Pacific near the western Aleutians, continues in a southeasterly direction, and ends in the last two islands of the Hawaiian chain, Maui and Hawaii. This chain of peaks is called the Emperor Seamounts. The seamounts are a long series of extinct volcanoes that have erupted and then gone dormant in sequence from north to south. They seem to have emerged from a great crack in the crust through which magma has continually reached the surface. It is as if the train of volcanoes marks a single spot in the crust through which magma has been able to reach the crustal surface— the bottom of the sea—as the Pacific plate has slowly turned on an axis, sliding over the mantle.

Geologists call this kind of leakage to the surface a *plume*. Other plumes may exist in other parts of the world in other plates. The evidence for the plume that formed the Emperor Seamounts and Hawaii, however, is the most easily read. The oldest volcanoes in the chain are the most northerly. Only two active volcanoes, the newest in the chain, still erupt. They are Kilauea and Mauna Loa, both on Hawaii, the most southerly island. In addition, the Emperor Seamounts are offset, rather than in a straight line. This may indicate the gradual turning of the Pacific plate in a counterclockwise direction.

Yet Hawaii and the Emperor Seamounts do not furnish the only clue to the tectonic plate theory. The fracture zones of the eastern Pacific may also be explained by such crustal movement. Despite their name, the fracture zones are not the focus of earthquakes, and they do not leak volcanic magma to the surface. Instead they seem to be cracks in the ocean floor caused by the slow turning of the Pacific plate. Geologists who believe in the tectonic plate theory think similar fracture zones in other plates, recently discovered, help to confirm this.

Not all the boundaries of crustal plates are marked by islands and trenches, however. In the Middle East rising mountains, volcanoes, and very active earth faults with many earthquakes seem to indicate plate borders. In the Atlantic the Mid-Atlantic Ridge seems to mark the separation between the American and Eurasian plates and the African plate. The Mid-Atlantic Ridge probably is caused by the upwelling of a convection current.

Here, however, a new factor has come into play. The flow of material to the crest of the Mid-Atlantic Ridge moves from east to west and west to east, rather than north and south, as it does in the Pacific. The material surging toward the surface of the earth seems to be spreading in opposing directions toward the continents. Geologists call this phenomenon *sea-floor spreading*. Sea-floor spreading seems to be taking place in various parts of the ocean. The East Pacific Rise, for example, is apparently being formed in the same way as the Mid-Atlantic Ridge, and spreading has also been found along other ridges and rises on the ocean floor.

The knowledge of sea-floor spreading, and, what is more

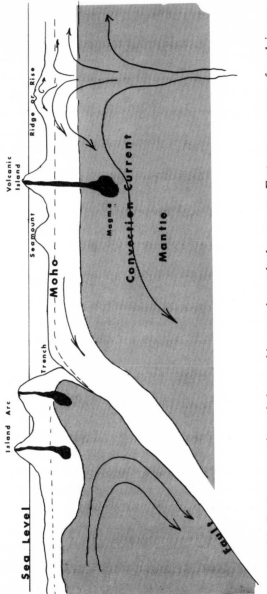

An idealized cross-section of the earth's crust beneath the oceans. Features are never found in exactly this relationship or so close together and are grouped in this drawing to make it possible to get them all on one page.

important, the theory of plate tectonics, renewed marine geologists' interest in a companion theory, that of *continental drift*. Such a theory was proposed in 1915 by a German meteorologist, Alfred Wegener, in a book called *The Origin of Continents and Oceans*. In it Wegener said that the earth's continents were once a single unit, but that over millions of years they had broken apart and drifted away from each other like floating islands.

Wegener's theory, in turn, was based on an earlier work by an American geologist, Frank B. Taylor. Between 1908 and 1910 Taylor suggested that the continents had once been joined together, but had slowly moved apart. Yet even Taylor's idea was not completely original. As early as the seventeenth century a Frenchman, François Placet, proposed that North and South America once had been joined to Europe and Africa by "land bridges." The bridges, according to Placet, had disappeared during the forty days of flood described in the Bible in the story of Noah and the ark.

Unlike Placet, both Wegener and Taylor based their writings on geologic principles. Taylor, for example, pointed out that samples of rock taken from the opposing coasts of Africa and South America were similar. He also noted that the continents were composed of materials lighter than those of the ocean floors. This, he said, would make it possible for continents to float and move about.

As sometimes happens in science, neither Wegener's nor Taylor's writings received much support when they were first published. Many geologists ridiculed Wegener's suggestions, and when he died in 1930, while on an expedition to Greenland, his theory was still in disrepute.

Increasing evidence supporting the theory of continental drift developed after World War II, however, as more and more knowledge of the sea floor was obtained. With studies of sea-floor spreading, the Mid-Atlantic Ridge, deep ocean trenches, and earthquake faults, information began to accumulate. Plate tectonics added additional credence to the possibility that the continents had once been one. Support for Wegener's theory continued to grow until today many geologists are convinced that continental drift is a reality and that once, perhaps 200 million years ago, the five continents were a single protocontinent called *Pangaea* (a word derived from the Greek, meaning "all lands").

This single continent was surrounded by a single world ocean, which covered the rest of the earth's surface. This world ocean has been called *Panthalassa* ("all seas"). About 135 million years ago the great landmass broke apart and formed two continents, Laurasia and Gondwanaland. Laurasia included most of what is now North and South America, Europe, and a large part of Asia. Gondwanaland made up the rest of the earth's land surface. The names are derived from present-day geologic formations, Laurentia (the area's ancient name) in Canada and Gondwana in India. Both are very ancient rock beds.

Sixty-five million years ago Laurasia divided into Europe, Asia, and North and South America. Gondwanaland became Africa, India, Australia, and Antarctica. Since then these bodies have gradually moved apart until they reached their present position on the earth's surface, India moving so that it touched the Asian continent. In another 50 million years they will have moved even farther apart, with some exceptions. Australia, for example, probably will have

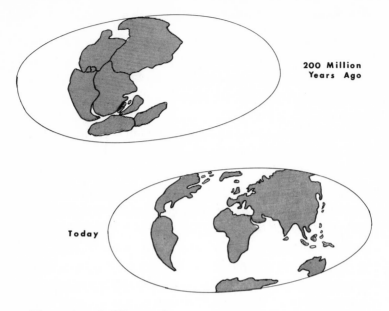

200 Million
Years Ago

Today

The projected difference between the earth's land surface today and 200 million years ago, showing the effect of continental drift. The map of 200 million years ago is inferred from present-day geological studies. The shape of the earth is exaggerated to give the continents proper perspective.

drifted north, like India, to touch the southern coast of Asia.

If the theory of continental drift could be proved correct, scientists felt it would help to explain some of the mysteries of the continents and the seas; some, but not all. One of these mysteries is the great age difference between continental rocks and the bottom of the oceans. Rocks in some parts of the continents are twice as old as the average age of the deep ocean bottom.

Still another puzzle is the coming and going of ice ages. The earth has been both warmer and cooler in the past. We live in one of its warmer intervals. Ten thousand years ago our planet was much colder than it is today. Ice, often as much as a mile thick, lay over large parts of North America, and where a single sheet of ice did not cover the land, individual glaciers often straddled mountains and valleys. Even near the equator the earth was far different in climate from what it is now. A similar series of events seems to have affected the Southern Hemisphere as well.

No one yet knows why the ice formed or why it receded, but geologic studies indicate clearly that a series of ice ages happened at fairly regular intervals. Whatever caused them, their effect was to turn much of the oceans' waters into ice and thus to lower the seas' level over the entire earth.

Some geologists speculate that these variations in the level of the seas are responsible for the odd flat tops of guyots. Their theory is that guyots once were ordinary seamounts, peaked and conical in shape. As the ice ages turned water from the oceans into ice, lowering the oceans' level, some seamounts reared their heads above the water. They then suffered from erosion and were planed flat by waves. Other geologists, however, contend that guyots are extinct volcanoes. Having once erupted in the ocean above sea level, they say, the guyots have gradually been lowered below the waves by sea-floor spreading, much as the volcanoes that form the bases for coral atolls seem to have gradually dropped lower and lower into the ocean.

Ice ages have also had their effect on the shorelines of the continents, exposing and covering them at different times in the past. In general, however, the outlines of the continents have remained remarkably the same since they first began to evolve as separate bodies of land.

One notable exception may be the west coast of North America. The East Pacific Rise runs north along the coast of Central America, into the Gulf of California, and then disappears under the North American continent. Approximately where it ends, the San Andreas Fault begins. The fault runs generally north and south through California, finally reentering the sea near Cape Mendocino, where it seems to join the Mendocino Fracture Zone.

It is probable, although not certain, geologists say, that the frequent earthquakes along the San Adreas Fault are

The general location of the San Adreas Fault of California, with several subsidiary connecting faults shown. There are many other smaller and less active faults in California not shown on this map.

really the result of the shifting and moving of the East Pacific Rise beneath the North American continent. The East Pacific Rise is the eastern boundary of the Pacific plate. What seems to have happened is that the continent has drifted out over the rise and is now being affected by this buried plate boundary. The upwelling of convection currents at the boundary of the American and Pacific plates may be affecting the land above it, or there may be a volcanic plume like the one that created Hawaii beneath this portion of the continent. Several volcanoes lie in the northeast corner of California. Thermal activity has also been found not far from Cape Mendocino in central California. Some geologists also believe the thermal activity around Yellowstone National Park in the northwestern part of the United States is an indication of another volcanic plume, long ago overridden by the westward movement of the North American continent.

One other mystery of the deep-sea bottom is unexplained by any of these suggestions and theories, however. It is the difference in magnetic alignment of rocks in the sea floor. A simple pocket compass shows the earth has a magnetic field. The earth is, in fact, a giant bar magnet, with the rocks of its crust magnetically aligned north and south. These rocks became so aligned when hot volcanic rock cooled to below a certain temperature, called the *Curie point*. Below this point particles permanently align themselves in the same direction as the earth's north-and-south magnetic poles. Since the rocks' magnetic polarity does not shift once the alignment has taken place, one might suppose that the direction of such alignment would be universal all over the earth's surface, but it is not.

By dragging magnetometers behind ships at sea, scientists have discovered that not all of the sea floor is of the same alignment. Instead, alignment varies in a regular pattern. If these variations are mapped, they show bands of rocks in which the alignment is directly opposite to nearby bands. In other words, the magnetic polarity of the earth has shifted from time to time in the past, and measurement of the polarity of different rock samples will show where the north and south poles were at different times in the past.

Dr. L. W. Morley of the Canadian Geological Survey and other marine geologists suggest that differences in alignment came about because of sea-floor spreading. As the sea floor spreads, they say, hot material wells up along plate boundaries and is warm enough to exceed the Curie point. When the material cools, its magnetic alignment is fixed, the direction of that alignment depending on the earth's polarity.

Neither Dr. Morley nor other scientists know why the earth's magnetic polarity has varied in the past, but in 1963 Dr. Morley found matching zones of polarity on opposite sides of undersea rises, establishing that different zones of alignment can be matched across opposing sides of plate boundaries where the sea floor is spreading.

This discovery helps to prove that sea-floor spreading is taking place and that it is taking place at a regular, measurable rate. Along some plate boundaries the spreading seems to occur uniformly on either side of the boundary. On others the sea floor seems to be spreading only in a single direction. To look at this another way, imagine that along some ridges in the ocean the earth's crust is being pushed in opposite directions, and that along others one side of the ridge seems to be stationary while the other side is being pushed away from it.

Of course such changes are taking place very slowly in our time, not more than an inch or two a year. In geologic time, time measured on the lifetime of the whole earth, however, such movement of the crust is rapid. The estimated age of the earth is about 4.5 billion years. If this period could be turned into a single day, it would mean that one second of the day would equal fifty thousand years of our time, one minute would equal 3 million years, and one hour would equal 180 million years. In such a reckoning man's time on earth would probably come to less than a second, his recorded history to an even briefer time. One hour on this great time clock equals the age of the ocean floors.

If we could see the entire earth's history as a single day, we would see sudden, immense changes. The continents would move; ice would cover the earth and recede within hours; the seas would rise and fall; mountains would erupt suddenly upward and then fall and become the bottoms of lakes or the edges of seas. A vast chain of events would be compressed into a shattering series of changes.

Although we will never see this happen, we do know now that it has taken place. The earth is a constantly evolving planet, and we are only just beginning to understand how some of these momentous changes came about. And we are only now starting to realize that the bottom of the sea will help to tell us how they occurred. As our understanding grows, we can be only more in awe of the power and beauty of the forces that have created the world on which we live.

Chapter 3

THE MOHOLE

One day in 1952 two scientists of the United States Office of Naval Research, Gordon Lill and Carl Alexis, were busily sorting applications from scientists seeking money with which to carry out research projects. It was their job to place the applications in various piles, depending on the category of science into which the proposals fell. After they had worked for a time, the two scientists found they had accumulated a sizable pile that they could label only as miscellaneous. As a joke, they decided they would create an organization to deal with such subjects.

The joke gradually expanded. It soon became a "society" divided into "sections" to "deal" with "trivia," "calamities," "visitors from outer space," and the like. The society even decided to issue an annual award, to be called "The Albatross Award" (apparently a reference to the albatross mentioned in Samuel Taylor Coleridge's famous poem *The*

Rime of the Ancient Mariner). The Miscellaneous Society, later to be called the American Miscellaneous Society, and still later simply AMSOC, had few fixed rules of order. It met infrequently, usually when its members were attending another scientific meeting, or on special occasions at the Cosmos Club, an exclusive Washington, D.C., eating, drinking, and social establishment. The society had no officers and few requirements for membership. Most of its members, however, were earth scientists. The topics they discussed at their meetings covered a wide range of subjects, and no idea was too unusual to be considered. One, for instance, was a proposal to tow an iceberg from the Arctic Sea to the coast of southern California, there to be melted and used as a source of water.

AMSOC continued as a private joke until 1957. In March of that year eight of its members were gathered in La Jolla, California, as part of a panel to consider projects submitted (in all seriousness) by earth scientists. After a day during which sixty projects were examined, the AMSOC members went to the home of Walter Munk, a Scripps Institution of Oceanography scientist, for a social hour and society meeting. During the meeting Dr. Munk pointed out that none of the projects discussed earlier in the day by the panel was really fundamental to a better understanding of the earth as a whole. He suggested AMSOC should promote a project that took this into consideration.

Then Harry Hess—the same Harry Hess mentioned in Chapter One—now chairman of the Department of Geology at Princeton University in New Jersey—added a thought. Why not, he said, drill a hole through the crust of the earth where it is thinnest—under the oceans—into the mantle?

Dr. Hess pointed out that although magma may come from the mantle, it reaches the surface of the earth "contaminated" by its passage through the crust. It would be far better, he said, to obtain a "pure" sample by drilling directly into the mantle.

Hess also had another idea. Why not, he said, turn the project over to AMSOC? After all, it had considered wilder schemes. The others at the meeting liked the suggestion. They discussed it a little more, but postponed their decision for a month. Then the AMSOC members convened again at Munk's home and appointed Gordon Lill, one of the society's founders, as chairman of the project. They also appointed a committee, later to be called the Deep Sea Drilling Committee, composed mostly of geologists and oceanographers, to assist him.

A few weeks later, now more serious than humorous, the Deep Sea Drilling Committee met at the Cosmos Club. That they should now consider the idea more than a joke must be viewed against the background of the times. The intense scientific rivalry between the United States and Russia had just begun, in part because of the race to create and explode a hydrogen bomb, in part because of competition in space flight. Science was a subject with which few government officials and members of Congress were familiar. They did know, however, that this country lagged in scientific development, and they were willing to consider almost any idea as a way of pulling abreast of the Russians.

The National Academy of Sciences and other scientific organizations had helped to create the new National Science Foundation as a way to fund money for scientific projects. Congress was willing to vote it large amounts of money.

Moreover, the idea of drilling deep into the center of the earth, if not often discussed among scientists, was not new. As early as 1881 the famous British naturalist Charles Darwin had suggested drilling a deep hole in a coral atoll in the Pacific. Darwin's plan evolved from his theory that coral atolls, peculiar circular-shaped islands, were made of the skeletons of corals, minute sea creatures, heaped up through many generations on old, extinct, sunken volcanic islands. This could be proved, he said, if a hole could be bored through the coral to reach the volcanic rock beneath.

In 1897 the Royal Society of England tried to drill such a hole on the coral atoll Funafuti in the Ellice Islands. The drillers reached a depth of 1,140 feet before they gave up. They were unable to strike volcanic rock.

In 1902 an American, G. K. Gilbert, director of the Carnegie Institution of Washington, D.C., proposed drilling a deep hole somewhere on the North American continent to study the lower depths of the continental crust. He was given a small amount of money by the Carnegie Institution to find a possible site for such a hole, but after several surveys abandoned the idea without doing any drilling.

In 1939 Dr. T. A. Jaggar, famous volcanologist and founder of the volcano observatory on the Hawaiian Islands, suggested that a number of old warships be tied together and towed to sea to make a drilling platform with which to drill into the mantle. Dr. Jaggar, who had many innovative ideas in his long lifetime, said the oil industry could provide the technical knowledge needed for the drilling operation, and he forwarded the idea to the International Union of Geodesy and Geophysics. Unfortunately, Dr. Jaggar was ahead of his time, so nothing ever came of his plan.

In the past there had also been several fanciful fictional ideas for exploring the center of the earth. In the nineteenth century the French science-fiction writer Jules Verne wrote a novel called *A Journey to the Center of the Earth,* which recounts the story of how several men travel down the conduit of an extinct volcano to reach a sea deep in the center of the planet. After various adventures they are blown back to the surface by a volcanic explosion.

Sir Arthur Conan Doyle, the author of the Sherlock Holmes stories, played with the idea, too, in a story entitled "When the Earth Screamed." In it he told of firing a needle of considerable size into the center of the earth to reach the mantle, whereupon the earth "screamed like an animal." Edgar Rice Burroughs, the author of the Tarzan stories, also treated the center of the earth as a habitable place in a book written in this century called *At the Earth's Core.*

The first realistic approach to the problem of drilling deeply into the crust appears to have been made in 1953 by Dr. Maurice Ewing of the Lamont-Doherty Geological Observatory in New York. Several times during the 1950's Dr. Ewing suggested that deep drilling of the crust was not only possible but also necessary if we were to understand more about the composition of our planet.

A similar but separate suggestion was made in the October 12, 1956, issue of *Science* magazine, the official journal of the American Association for the Advancement of Science, by Dr. Frank B. Estabrook of the Basic Research Branch of the United States Army. Dr. Estabrook's plan, however, was to drill from an island, rather than at sea, as Dr. Jaggar had proposed.

The first deep-sea drilling *was* done on islands in a renewed effort to prove that Darwin's theory about coral atolls was correct. In the 1930's the Japanese sank a shaft 1,416 feet into an island off Japan, but did not succeed in reaching volcanic rock. The task was taken up again in 1952 by Gordon Lill and two associates, Harry Ladd and Joshua Tracey. Before the nuclear bomb tests on Bikini atoll, they drilled an even deeper hole, also without finding volcanic rock. Several months later, however, the same scientists tried again and, this time, finally reached *basalt,* a volcanic rock, at 4,222 feet.

There was a basic difference between these efforts, however, and those that would be needed to drill through the crust under the ocean to reach the mantle. The Bikini drilling was done on land. Land offers a stable drilling platform. In any attempt to drill in the deep sea, one would first have to penetrate an average depth of close to fourteen thousand feet of seawater. Drilling would also have to be done from the deck of a ship, floating on the surface of the ocean, subjected to winds, waves, and other natural forces.

Also, no one knew how long it would take to drill a hole through three miles of crust after the ocean bottom was reached. Best estimates were at least two years. To provision a ship and keep it over the drill hole for that length of time presented sizable logistic problems. In addition, if the drill string had to be removed from the hole, it would then have to be guided back into place again. No one knew how such a thing was to be accomplished.

Moreover, no one knew how expensive the drill project would be, but obviously it might be quite costly. But there seemed to be hope for the latter problem.

The National Science Foundation seemed the most likely

source of money for such scientific research. Even so, AMSOC was an unlikely organization to request such funds. Realizing this, the members decided to seek the support and endorsement of older and more serious scientific groups, and they quickly introduced resolutions asking for such assistance. Somewhat to their surprise, they found enthusiastic support in many places. At one international meeting they even got the unwitting help of a Russian scientist, who arose to announce that the Russians already were at work on a similar project. (If they were, no evidence of such a plan has ever materialized.)

Even the National Academy of Sciences took an interest in the project, partly because five of the members of the Deep Sea Drilling Committee were also members of the academy. In a short time the academy admitted AMSOC to membership, giving it the endorsement of the most highly regarded scientific organization in the United States, and on April 2, 1958, the academy filed an application with the National Science Foundation on behalf of AMSOC seeking $30,000. This money would be used to carry out a feasibility study to see if the plan would work. By this time, too, the project had received a name. Because it was intended to penetrate the Mohorovičić discontinuity, it was dubbed *Mohole*.

At the same time the AMSOC members found technological help in the petroleum industry, as Dr. Jaggar had predicted. Four oil companies, Continental, Union, Shell, and Superior, had recently joined forces to explore the offshore continental shelf of the United States for oil deposits. To carry out such exploration, the four companies jointly bought an old navy freight barge and outfitted it with a drilling rig. The vessel was christened *CUSS I,* a combination of the first letters of the four companies' names.

Not only did *CUSS I* have a drilling rig aboard, it also had a positioning system, devised by Willard Bascom, an engineer with experience in geology. The system consisted of four huge two-hundred-horsepower outboard motors attached to the four corners of the barge and controlled by a single "joystick." By moving the stick, an operator could constantly shift the position of the vessel bearing the drilling rig to keep it over the drill hole. A circle of buoys was set around the drilling vessel, and the operator used them as guides to determine the vessel's proper location.

With their National Science Foundation funds, the members of the AMSOC Deep Sea Drilling Committee leased *CUSS I* and began a survey of possible sites at which to sink an experimental hole into the ocean bottom. Banking on the experience of the oil companies, they decided this should be on the continental shelf, the extension of the continental land surface that extends out beneath the ocean. The water depth at such a point in the ocean would not be as great as it would be in the place where a final Mohole would be drilled, but they could obtain valuable experience for a later, full-scale attempt to reach the mantle.

Various sites were surveyed, and one off the coast of Lower California was finally selected. Late in March, 1961, *CUSS I* was towed to a place in the ocean near Guadalupe Island where the water was about ten thousand feet deep. *CUSS I*'s drill string was lowered to the ocean bottom, and drilling operations began. Several drill holes were sunk during late March, culminating on April 6 with a hole 601 feet deep, the deepest point man had ever reached into the sea bottom at the time. Both the positioning system and the extended drill string worked well.

By this time the Mohole had begun to attract national and international attention. With additional funds from the National Science Foundation, the former joke of the American Miscellaneous Society had become a serious scientific endeavor, so serious that the successful completion of the test Mohole brought a telegram of commendation from President John F. Kennedy.

The next step, however, lay beyond the capabilities of *CUSS I.* Bascom, who had become leader of the project, now proposed that the first Mohole be drilled in the deep sea off Hawaii, but this could not be done without a larger drill platform, more extensive drilling equipment, and additional money. The original $30,000 had long since been spent, and a great deal more was needed to proceed with the project. The National Science Foundation pledged additional funds for the construction of a larger vessel capable of carrying out at least two and a half years of continuous drilling.

After months of consideration, a contract for the expanded Mohole project was awarded to the Brown & Root Company of Houston, Texas, a firm with extensive oil-drilling experience. After some study the contracting company issued specifications for the new Mohole ship. It was not only to be considerably larger than *CUSS I,* it was also to be a great deal more expensive. The company proposed the construction of a ten-thousand-ton vessel 234 by 250 feet, which would rest on six 29-foot steel columns. These, in turn, would be based on two steel hulls, each 370 feet long and 35 feet in diameter. The ship, once launched,

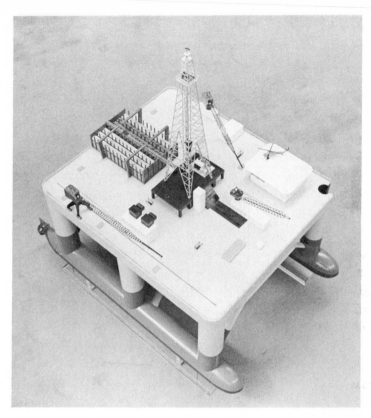

Model of the Mohole drilling ship which was never built because of its high cost and the decision to abandon the Mohole project.   *Courtesy National Science Foundation*

would be driven to the drill site by motors in the hulls with propellers attached to their sterns. At the drill site the cylindrical hulls would be filled with water, which would lower the main deck of the ship to water level.

Like *CUSS I* the new Mohole ship would be kept in position over the drill hole by the system devised by Bascom.

The system had been refined and improved, however. Instead of an operator using a joystick, a computer would constantly monitor the ship's position. The computer would receive signals from a series of radar and sonar buoys moored both on and below the ocean's surface. Drilling would be carried out in the same way as had been done on *CUSS I,* by lowering a drill string through the water to the ocean bottom. From there drilling would continue until the crust had been penetrated. During the drilling, continuous cores of the ocean bottom, routed out by the drilling bit, would be brought to the surface for analysis and study.

Brown & Root's first estimate of the cost of the new Mohole vessel was $67,700,000, far more than had been appropriated in the past, either for that project or for any other scientific project. And the cost of it mounted quickly. It would finally reach $125 million.

This was the first and most important of numerous political and financial problems to be encountered by Project Mohole, problems having little to do with its scientific merits.

The number of opponents of the project in Congress began to grow. They attacked the support of the program by Texas congressmen, particularly Congressman Albert Thomas, who was chairman of a House of Representatives subcommittee considering money for the project. His opponents accused Congressman Thomas of favoring Brown & Root because it was a Texas firm, even though the company had previously carried out similar projects for the government without difficulty.

It was also alleged that President Lyndon Johnson, who had succeeded President Kennedy after his assassination, and who was also from Texas, had used his influence to have the Houston company take over the management of Mohole, but that accusation was never proved.

Congressman Thomas died shortly after the project came before his subcommittee, and the chairmanship went to Congressman Joe L. Evins of Tennessee. Congressman Evins, a longtime foe of Mohole, quickly recommended that the entire project be shelved and the House of Representatives concurred. Despite the success of the Lower California tests, on August 24, 1966, Project Mohole was formally put to rest.

Project Mohole was dead. Or was it?

If it was not exactly alive, its ghost survived in a new project, the Joint Oceanographic Institutions for Deep Earth Sampling (JOIDES). JOIDES was a combination of four oceanographic institutions: Lamont-Doherty Geological Observatory in New York, Woods Hole Oceanographic Institution in Massachusetts, Scripps Institution of Oceanography in California, and the University of Miami in Florida. Even while Project Mohole was under way, these four institutions had begun to consider a less ambitious deep-sea drilling program.

The JOIDES plan was to drill in the deep ocean, not in a single place, as had been the case with Project Mohole, but in many places around the world with a drilling rig to be carried aboard an oceangoing ship, a ship smaller and less expensive than the Mohole vessel.

The JOIDES plan had originally been proposed by Dr. Cesare Emiliani of the University of Miami. He urged drilling on a limited scale in the Caribbean Sea and Atlantic Ocean. Dr. Emiliani's plan was referred to a committee

nicknamed LOCO, which included two scientists from each
of the four institutions. Later Princeton University was
added to the group because Dr. Harry Hess worked there.
LOCO failed to become a reality, so a second group called
CORE was formed. It was to have examined the sediments
taken from the Mohole when coring began. It, too, failed
with the death of Mohole. A third effort by the University
of Miami, to explore the ocean floor off the island of
Jamaica in the Caribbean, also came to nothing.

Finally, while the Congressional dispute over Mohole was
at its height, the four members of JOIDES signed a contract
in May, 1964, agreeing that any one of them might contract
for the other three for drilling operations on a ship to be
leased for that purpose. Ultimately, this was to be Scripps.
The JOIDES group thereupon leased the *Caldrill,* a ship
similar to *CUSS I.* With it, experimental drilling was carried
out in 1965 in the Atlantic at shallow depths along the
continental shelf.

Thus, when Mohole collapsed and died, the technology
it had produced and the legacy of drilling the sea bottom
passed to the JOIDES group. On June 24, 1966, Scripps,
acting on behalf of the other three institutions, signed a
contract with the National Science Foundation for $12,-
600,000 to be used in extended deep-sea drilling over the
following eighteen months. In another form, Mohole lived
again. Deep-sea drilling was about to take place once more.

First, however, the expensive ruins of Project Mohole
had to be salvaged. The man selected to do this job was
Archie McLerran, an engineer with years of experience in
the oil-drilling business. McLerran was faced with more
than $60 million in contracts signed by the National Science

Foundation in anticipation of the beginning of Mohole. This figure was gradually reduced to about $25 million, and some of the equipment and contracts originally designed for Mohole were diverted to JOIDES.

Some of the technology that was passed on included the idea of dynamic positioning, logging winches, the design of the drill pipe to be used, the method of drill pipe inspection, and the proposed method of reentering a hole previously drilled. Thus, Mohole was not a costly financial failure, but rather the real beginning of reaching to the bottom of the sea and beyond.

Chapter 4

JOIDES AND THE
GLOMAR CHALLENGER

The first task of the JOIDES group was to find a ship that would do the job of drilling into the deep-sea bottom. No such vessel existed when the original founders of the Joint Oceanographic Institutions for Deep Earth Sampling Project began to examine the technical problems involved in the exploration of the deep-sea floor.

There had been additional sea-bottom drillings since the first Mohole test shafts had been sunk off Lower California, but these had been carried out by oil companies. The original *CUSS I* had been succeeded by *CUSS II*. *CUSS II*, in turn, had been followed by a series of specially constructed drilling ships that would eventually grow to thirteen in number. Designed to drill the ocean floor along the continental shelf of North America for deposits of undersea oil, all these vessels had been built by Global Marine, Inc., of Los Angeles, a firm created by some of the original oil companies that had built *CUSS I* and *CUSS II*. None of the ships, however, had been specifically designed for the kind of job planned by JOIDES.

It was to Global Marine, then, that the planners of JOIDES turned. They asked the National Science Foundation to allow them to contract with the Los Angeles shipbuilding company for a new vessel equipped with drilling equipment capable of reaching the sea bottom far from land.

JOIDES intended to lease the vessel for the duration of the deep-sea drilling project. The members of JOIDES also agreed that Scripps Institution of Oceanography should be the prime contractor for such a scientific expedition, but that scientists from other institutions in the United States and abroad could serve aboard the ship.

The National Science Foundation agreed to the proposal and provided the necessary money. On October 18, 1967, the keel for the new ship was laid at the Levington Shipbuilding Company yards in Orange, Texas. The new ship was similar in design to earlier Global Marine vessels, but it also had some significant differences.

First, it was larger than any of the company's previous ships. Second, it was specifically designed for very deep sea drilling. Third, its primary mission was the collection, storage, and examination of cores from holes in the ocean floor.

The new ship displaced 10,500 tons. It was 400 feet long and 65 feet wide. It looked somewhat like an oil tanker with its superstructure and pilot house near its stern. Here the resemblance to a conventional ship ended. Mounted midship was a 142-foot drilling derrick similar to, but larger than, many conventional land-based oil-drilling rigs. Beneath it, running completely through the ship, was a 20-by-22-foot well, called the *moon pool*. (The name originated, for uncertain reasons, among drilling crews on Texas tower platforms in the Santa Barbara Channel off California.) Through this moon pool the drill string was lowered to the bottom.

So that the drill string would be secured, the moon pool contained a collar through which the pipe would run. The collar would hold the drill string in place, but would also allow some movement or play after it had been extended beneath the ship. Beside the derrick tower on the ship's main deck was a specially designed pipe rack capable of holding 24,000 feet of five-inch, seawater-resistant drill pipe divided into 45-foot sections. The pipe was to be assembled by an automatic racker into lengths about equal to the height of the tower. An additional 12,000 feet of pipe was also to be stored below deck.

Like *CUSS I,* the new vessel had a dynamic positioning system capable of keeping it always over the drill hole. The new system, however, was more efficient than the old. Instead of the four outboard motors used on *CUSS I,* the new ship would be kept on position by the twin propellers of its engines and by pumps capable of forcing water through ports in both the bow and stern of its hull. These pumps were powered by the ship's twelve diesel electric engines.

In addition, the new positioning system would not normally be operated by hand. Instead a small on-board computer did the job. The computer received information from the ring of above- and below-surface radar and sonar buoys, and it ordered the thrusters to increase or decrease their jets of water to maintain position in relation to the markers. The computer control could be overridden by a manual control, if necessary.

The positioning system had another new device. At the bow of the vessel was to be a radio mast, which would per-

A technician climbs ladder to perform maintenance on the *Glomar Challenger*'s satellite navigation antenna.

Courtesy Scripps Institution of Oceanography

mit the ship to receive information from stationary navigation satellites lofted into space by the United States. This
permitted very accurate determination of the ship's position.

The vessel's planners did not underestimate the problem
of lowering ten to twelve thousand feet of pipe through the
ocean to the bottom. The ship's derrick and winches were
capable of lifting a million pounds, although it was not
expected that this weight would ever be suspended beneath
it. A drill string twelve thousand feet long, however, would
weigh about a third of this amount, approximately 300,000
pounds.

Cores obtained by the drill string's coring device would
be brought from the bottom of any holes drilled in the sea
floor to the deck of the ship by a long wire, which was fed
down the center of the pipe and hauled back aboard by a
power winch. The coring device would be able to obtain a
maximum of thirty feet of bottom at one time.

The ship had room for twenty-three scientists and techni-
cians, forty-five crewmen, including fourteen men to operate
the drilling rig, and nine stewards. It could remain at sea
for an average of two months, after which most of the
scientific personnel aboard would be changed. The crew
would remain on board for longer periods of time, however.

There remained the problem of giving the ship a name.
It was decided to call the new vessel the *Glomar Challenger*.
The first part of the name came from the ship's builder
and owner, Global Marine. The second was meant to sig-
nify a relationship with the first *Challenger* and its worldwide exploration of the oceans. The *Glomar Challenger*
was to take a similar worldwide look at the bottom of the
sea.

Although the mission of the two vessels was similar, they themselves were not. It is interesting to compare the two. The first *Challenger* was powered by steam and sail. A converted steam corvette of the British Royal Navy, it was not specifically designed for oceanic exploration, but was refitted for its task. For example, all but two of its eighteen guns had to be removed before it could be outfitted for scientific purposes.

The original *Challenger* was also much smaller than its twentieth-century namesake, almost half its length and beam. The *Challenger* displaced five times less tonnage and carried a crew only about half that of the drilling ship.

The original *Challenger* maintained its stations while making observations by using a combination of its engine and sails. It had no dynamic positioning system.

Scientists on the first *Challenger* were interested in the sea bottom, of course, but their primary mission was a study of the sea in general, its below-surface life, its shores, winds, waves, currents, and a host of other things. Both ships were prepared to return specimens and samples to shore, but their cargoes of scientific treasures were to be of different kinds. The *Challenger*'s goal was to find out as much as possible about all parts of the sea and to return to land as many samples of rare and unusual sea creatures as it could. The *Glomar Challenger*'s task was to recover cores from the bottom of the sea from as many different places as possible. It was also to plumb to depths in the ocean bottom impossible to reach with conventional coring devices.

The two ships did have a common objective: the exploration of a great unknown. When the first *Challenger* put to sea, large areas of the world's oceans were an uncharted mystery. When the *Glomar Challenger* began its voyages, the limited samples of the sea floor obtained by oceanographic vessels were only a scratching at the surface of the world's last frontier. The *Glomar Challenger* was about to enter a world known only by inference and indirection.

The *Glomar Challenger*'s hull was completed early in 1968, and on March 23 of that year Mrs. William A. Nierenberg, wife of the president of the Scripps Institution of Oceanography, smashed a bottle of champagne against its bow to christen and launch it officially. Five months later, on August 11, 1968, the vessel, now completely outfitted, sailed from Texas into the Gulf of Mexico on its maiden voyage or, as its journeys were to be called, its first *leg,* Leg I.

Leg I was intended to be a shakedown cruise both for the ship and for its drilling equipment. The scientists planned to lower the drill string into the relatively calm and shallow waters of the Gulf. Later they would move into the rougher Atlantic Ocean.

On August 19, 1968, the *Glomar Challenger* heaved to over a previously charted series of low undersea hills called the Sigsbee Knolls. The Sigsbee Knolls had been selected as a drill site for several reasons. They were at a depth similar to the average depth of the ocean. They were close to the coast from which the *Glomar Challenger* had been launched. Finally, the knolls were believed to be a series of salt domes, upwellings of the earth's crust that might indicate the presence of oil and natural gas.

As soon as the ship had put out its surface and subsurface buoys, the job of lowering the drill string began.

The *Glomar Challenger*'s drilling crew went on deck and prepared to fit the first sections of pipe into the rig.

Drilling on the *Glomar Challenger* is not much different from drilling on land. The operation is based on the simple principle that it is necessary to turn a drill bit around and around if it is to cut away the material through which it is drilling. Both in oil drilling on land and in drilling at sea aboard the *Glomar Challenger,* this is accomplished by fitting the drill pipe, whatever its length, into a heavy round turntable called a *rotary platform.* As an engine turns the platform, it turns the entire drill string and the drill bit.

First, however, the drill string must be made up, or assembled. Drill pipe is put together in sections by the ship's automatic pipe racker. The pipe is then pulled aloft inside the ship's drilling derrick by a heavy block and tackle, called the *crown block,* until it is vertical, rather than horizontal. The bottom end of the drill string—the first section of pipe containing the drill bit—is then fitted through the rotary platform and lowered through the moon pool until all but the upper end of the pipe has been so lowered. A coupling device, called a *bumper sub,* is then fitted around that end, and a second piece of pipe is lifted aloft and attached to the end of the first pipe.

This process continues until the crew has assembled the entire drill string and lowered it to the ocean bottom, a process that may take several hours, depending on the depth of water beneath the ship. Clamps are then fastened on the pipe to hold it tightly to the rotary platform, and the platform begins to turn. Far below, at the bottom of the sea, the drill bit also begins to turn.

Often, however, before he starts drilling, the drill-string

Crewmen bring in another 90-foot stand of drill pipe aboard the *Glomar Challenger*. The stand is hoisted by the elevators visible in the upper part of the picture. Connection will be made into the drill-pipe box visible on floor.

Courtesy Scripps Institution of Oceanography

operator will blow away some of the sea-bottom sediment with water jets in the sides of the drill string, for scientists are not always interested in the uppermost layers of the sea floor.

To tell the depth at which he is drilling, the drill-string operator watches dials that measure the length of the pipe being lowered to the bottom. He can also tell when the drill bit has reached the sea floor because of a sudden lightening on the drill string itself. The drill string represents a considerable weight, and as soon as it rests on the sea floor, there is a sudden lessening of the strain on the crown block.

In land drilling, of course, drilling starts when the first length of drill-string pipe is placed in the rotary platform and touches the earth beneath the derrick. Here the first assembly of a drill string may take only a short time because the rotary bit at the end of the string must grind its way through the earth for days, weeks, or months before it reaches depths equal to those necessary to reach the sea floor.

There is another big difference between land and sea drilling. Drilling on land requires the use of *liquid mud*. Liquid mud is just what its name implies, a very thin earth-and-water mixture, not much thicker than water. Liquid mud is usually made in a tank or open pit at the side of a land-based derrick and pumped down the drill hole as the drill bit turns.

There the liquid mud does three jobs. It helps keep the drill bit cool by drawing off the heat the drill bit's friction generates; it helps seal the sides of the hole against cave-ins; and it carries away rock and other debris from around the bit back to the surface. As the mud is pumped down the hole, it is eventually forced back to the surface, where it is passed through a screen to remove bits of rock and grit. Then it is pumped back down the hole again.

The *Glomar Challenger* carried liquid mud, but it was

seldom used because seawater served the same purpose.

The *Glomar Challenger*'s drill bit was also somewhat different from those used in land drilling. At first the "roughnecks" of the drilling crew used diamond-studded drill bits —tiny pieces of industrial diamonds fastened to the bit— but later they substituted tungsten-hardened steel rotary bits. The *Glomar Challenger*'s bits were also slightly wider than those used on land. This was to permit the bit to cut a path for the thirty-foot core tube lowered inside the drill pipe. As the bit cut its way into the sea bottom, it allowed the core tube to sink deeper and deeper into the layers under the sea floor.

When the core tube was filled, it was hauled back to the surface inside the drill pipe. The core contained a sample of all the layers in that particular section of the bottom.

As soon as one core tube was brought to the deck of the *Glomar Challenger,* a second tube could be lowered to take its place. Although a continuous core sample of the drill hole could be collected in this way, in practice coring was seldom done continuously. Instead, to minimize the number of times the drill string had to be stopped to allow another core tube to be sent to the bottom, coring was done at intervals determined by the *Glomar Challenger*'s scientific crew.

Of course, the technique described was used if everything went as it should. Not infrequently, however, things did not work out this way. The core sometimes got lost at the bottom of the drill string. The drill string itself sometimes broke. The drill bit became too dull to cut. To solve some of these difficulties, the drilling crew sometimes had to "fish" the bottom of the hole to retrieve broken pieces of equipment. More likely, however they had to remove the entire drill string from the hole and return it to the ship's deck.

In drilling on land, removing the drill string is often less difficult than at sea. The drill string is withdrawn from the hole, taken apart a section at a time, and reracked. A new bit is then fitted at the end of the drill string, and after assembly, the drill string is lowered back down the hole.

At sea, entry into the drill hole is much more difficult. Instead of lying just below the derrick, the drill hole is ten thousand feet or more away. Trying to fit a new drill bit back into the ten-inch hole in the sea bottom is a little like trying to thread a needle held ten feet from the eye.

Because of this, the designers of the *Glomar Challenger* planned a special reentry system. It required the use of a sixteen-foot cone surrounded by four sonar reflectors. The cone was pulled around under the keel of the ship to the moon pool before drilling began. There the drill string was fitted to the hole in the bottom of the cone. As the drill string was lowered to the bottom, the reentry cone was lowered with it. When they reached the bottom, the drill bit came out through the hole in the reentry cone and cut into the sediments. If, for some reason, the drill string had to be withdrawn, the reentry cone was left in place on the bottom. Then, when reentry was attempted, the sonar reflectors guided the drill string downward to a point directly over the reentry cone. Water jets at the bottom of the drill string helped to maneuver the long length of pipe horizontally until sonar indicated it was in the proper position. Then it was quickly lowered into the cone and back into the drill hole.

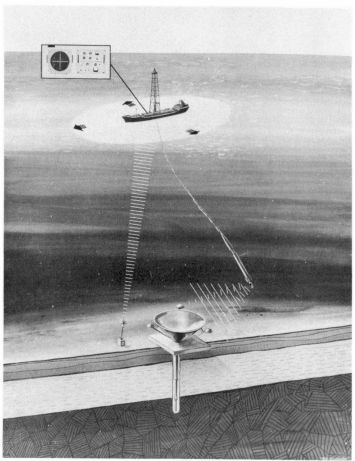

Deep Sea Drilling Project engineers responded to scientists' demands for a way to reenter a drilling hole by designing the system shown here. A sharp bit is being guided into a subsea core hole, using a high-resolution scanning sonar probe. The reentry cone, with its casing "stinger," was set on the ocean bottom during the previous drilling at this site. The ability to reenter the same hole and continue drilling makes it possible to penetrate through hard layers and deep into hard rock that will dull the drill bit so that it must be hauled up and replaced.

Courtesy Scripps Institution of Oceanography

However, this system of reentry was not attempted during the drilling of the first holes in the Sigsbee Knolls, nor for more than a year afterward. Instead, the drill crew and scientists aboard were chiefly concerned with reaching a sufficient depth in the sea bottom to remove sample cores. For over four days, while the ship's dynamic positioning system kept the *Glomar Challenger* directly above the drill hole, the drill string was kept lowered through 9,259 feet of water. The drill bit then ground its way through 2,528 feet of ocean bottom, making it possible to stop the drill string nine times and take core samples from the hole.

The scientists aboard sampled each of these cores in a way that was to become standard during succeeding legs of the *Glomar Challenger*'s voyages. As soon as a thirty-foot core tube was pulled back onto the ship, they took two *smear samples,* one at each end of the tube, by wiping glass plates over the open ends of the tube. Then they examined the samples under a microscope to see what, if anything, the core tube might contain in microfossils and other material. By identifying the fossils, they could date the sample and decide whether or not to take additional cores.

The core was then removed from the tube, separated into smaller sections, and cut in half to expose the entire sequence of undersea layers in the sample. If the scientists found the core to be of no immediate interest, they ordered it wrapped in plastic and placed in one of the *Glomar Challenger*'s special storage refrigerators.

These refrigerators were designed to keep the core samples moist until they could be removed from the vessel for storage and examination on land. If the *Glomar Challenger* was in the Pacific, the cores later went to the Scripps

Institution of Oceanography in La Jolla, California, the headquarters for the Deep Sea Drilling Project. If it was in the Atlantic, the ship took the cores to the Lamont-Doherty Geological Laboratory in New York.

Often, however, the scientists sampled and examined a core in detail right aboard the *Glomar Challenger*. First, they weighed it to determine its density. Then they might X-ray it to see some of its internal structure. Using a gamma radiation counter, the scientists might also measure the gamma radiation emissions to get an idea of the core's water content and porosity. Once the core was divided in half, one half would be carefully photographed while the second half was put in storage for safekeeping.

The scientists then began a series of microscopic examinations of the core's fossil content. This is a concern of the branch of geology known as *micropaleontology,* which is the study of the skeletons of the minute sea creatures that make up much of deep-sea sediments. To obtain samples, the scientists took small amounts of material from the core sections, washed the material carefully in water and hydrogen peroxide to free it from mud, and mounted the samples on glass microscope slides.

They then attempted to date and identify the fossils. Dating was accomplished through two methods of examination. The first was to measure their carbon 14 content. This process, developed by Nobel Prize winner Dr. Willard Libby, is based on the fact that carbon 14, an isotope of the carbon atom, changes into normal carbon at a fixed and measurable rate. By measuring the amount of carbon 14 in a fossil sample, it is possible to establish its age.

Dating also can be done by matching the fossil sample

with other previously identified and dated fossils of the same kind. Microscopic fossils exist in a vast variety—more than thirty thousand different species have been identified to date.

Fossils can also give clues to variations in climate. One minute organism with a shell, the *Globorotana truncatulinoides,* lives in both warm and cold water. In warm water its shell is curled counterclockwise; in cold water, clockwise. No one knows why. However, scientists do understand that the shells are an accurate reflection of variations in the temperature of ocean waters.

If carbon 14 cannot be used as a yardstick for age, oxygen content can. Like carbon, oxygen has an isotope, oxygen 18. Oxygen 18 is more likely to be present in the shells of marine animals that have lived in warm waters. Scientists have used such measurements to date the ice ages that have affected the earth in the past. From such studies they have concluded that the Pleistocene epoch, the last time when glaciers covered much of the earth, began over one million years ago. It was broken at intervals by warm periods which began about 536,000, 320,000, 175,000, and 20,000 years ago.

Scientists on the *Glomar Challenger* may also make chemical tests to analyze the content of core materials. This too helps to tell what has happened to the earth in the past.

These tests were made of the first series of cores recovered from the Sigsbee Knolls. They showed that the bottom of the sea in that part of the Gulf of Mexico was relatively young geologically. The tests also revealed evidence of both oil and gas, the first time petroleum had been found at such depths in the ocean.

Its tests complete, the *Glomar Challenger* sailed into the Atlantic to make a new series of borings of the bottom. Here the scientists were trying to find the depth and age of sediments along the flanks of the Mid-Atlantic Ridge. Toward the end of the legs sailed in the South Atlantic during 1968, they also drilled along the coasts of Africa and South America, looking for additional indications that these two continents once were joined together.

Then, passing through the Caribbean Sea, the *Glomar Challenger* used the Panama Canal to reach the Pacific. In this ocean the crew sank drill holes in many places: off the coast of North America, off Hawaii, in the central Pacific, around the island arcs of the western Pacific, and along the flanks of the East Pacific Rise. This work consumed the first eighteen months of the Deep Sea Drilling Project. Additional National Science Foundation money made a thirty-month extension of the project possible and permitted the *Glomar Challenger* to sail around the world, drilling again in the Atlantic and the Pacific, in the Mediterranean Sea, and in the Indian Ocean. Still another extension gave the ship a chance to explore the ocean bottom off the west coast of South America and around Antarctica.

Each time the *Glomar Challenger* reached port, usually about every fifty-five or sixty days, a new crew of scientists came aboard. The data they gathered were published in a long series of reports. By early 1974 the *Glomar Challenger* had drilled 468 holes at 318 different sites, cored 187,194 feet of sediment, of which 103,529 feet was safely on shore in storage, and traveled 165,353 nautical miles, more than six times around the world.

In so doing, the ship set at least three records. First, in

the Indian Ocean, it drilled 4,265 feet below the bottom of the sea, the deepest man has yet penetrated beneath the ocean. In the same body of water, the *Glomar Challenger* put down 22,192 feet of drill pipe, another new record for deep-sea drilling.

Finally, on December 25, 1970, for the first time, the ship's drilling crew was able to achieve reentry into a hole previously drilled. As the *Glomar Challenger* continued its drilling operations during 1969 and 1970, it became increasingly clear that reentry would be necessary to achieve greater drilling depths. The chief reason was that in many holes drilling could proceed easily only until a layer of *chert* was reached. Chert is a very hard rock much like porcelain in texture. It is so hard that it rapidly wore out the diamond bits first used in drilling. The tungsten roller bit later substituted could penetrate the material better, but even tungsten bits often began to dull after grinding against chert.

Without the ability to reenter the drill hole, drilling crews and scientists on the *Glomar Challenger* could only pull up the drill string, substitute a new bit for the dull one, and move on to a new station. It was important, therefore, to find out whether the system, which seemed theoretically possible, would work in practice. Designers of the system had estimated that it would take about fifteen hours to change a bit and reenter a hole. The test on Christmas Day, however, took longer than this because of several complications. A section of the drill pipe became dented and had to be returned to the ship's deck and replaced. A crewman was injured, further delaying the test. The sonar system used to position the drill string over the reentry cone failed temporarily. Then the sea rose, making it difficult to keep the *Glomar Challenger* on station over the hole.

Finally, just before eight o'clock on Christmas night, 1970, the drill string slipped back into the reentry cone and reentered the original drill hole. The crew lowered more than 10,000 feet of pipe to the sea bottom, an amount of pipe equal to 290,000 pounds. They began the coring and at last successfully lifted to the surface the first cores to be taken from a reentered drill hole. They had proved that the idea of reentering a hole only ten inches in diameter more than 10,000 feet below a swaying, bobbing platform on the surface of the ocean was practically possible.

Chapter 5

READING
THE CORES

It took twenty-three years to write the fifty volumes that record the discoveries of the voyage of the first *Challenger*. It may take even longer to analyze and chronicle the voyages of the *Glomar Challenger*. The more than 180,000 feet of cores gathered from the more than 450 holes drilled have accumulated so rapidly that they are far from being completely "read." The more than 350 scientists from the twenty-three nations that have taken part in the ship's explorations have much to learn before they know all the cores contain.

Although information is published at the end of each voyage, it is not a complete description of all that is in the cores of that particular leg. Moreover, no complete effort has yet been made to relate the findings of all voyages to one another.

Some basic information has begun to emerge from the

studies, however. Some of it is new knowledge. Much of it is confirmation of theories previously stated, particularly the theories of plate tectonics and continental drift. Confirmation comes from several different kinds of evidence. First, the cores show that sediments are thinnest in places where the sea floor is spreading away from ridges and rises. The sediments increase in depth as the distance away from these points increases. Because the depth of sediments is a measure of the age of the bottom, the youngest sea floor is constantly being created by spreading.

Equally important, no cores gathered anywhere in the ocean are as old as the cores taken from the continents, which has several important implications for the theory of plate tectonics. It means that no part of the ocean bottom is as old as parts of the continents. Instead, *all* the sea floor is younger than much of the continental surface of the earth.

If the continents are older than the sea floor, they must have been on earth for a long time, and they could well be the floating "islands" suggested in the thory of continental drift. Their shape also does not seem to have changed much since they first broke apart and began to move over the surface of the earth, shoved about by sea-floor spreading.

If this is true, it poses a new puzzle. If the continents are older than the sea bottom, what has happened to the sea floor that was present when the continents were first formed? It is no longer on the surface of the earth. It must have gone somewhere, but where? The most likely answer seems to be that it has been recycled back into the mantle at places where submarine trenches exist.

Wherever the bottom of the earth's primal seas has gone, it has been replaced by ocean floor that can be no more than 150 million years in age. Compared to the oldest rocks on the continents, which are 3.5 *billion* years old, the bottom of the sea is exceedingly young in geologic time. This fact indicates to geologists that the recycling to the ocean bottom takes place at a very rapid rate.

The cores also suggest some new ideas about the composition of the upper layers of the mantle and the lower layers of the crust. Both the crust and the mantle now seem to be more complex than was first supposed. It now seems likely that the upper levels of the mantle are divided into two parts, the *lithosphere* and the *asthenosphere*. The lithosphere seems to extend to the depth of the Moho discontinuity. It includes the brittle portion of the crust. It is the material in which the continents rest like islands—the portion that is being moved about by sea-floor spreading.

Below the Moho in the asthenosphere lie two other apparent discontinuities, both so far without names. The first is at about 250 miles, the second about 400 miles. The estimates of these depths are based on earthquake studies.

Geologists now believe that earthquakes take place in one of four different areas of the world: along the boundaries of tectonic plates, usually in association with volcanic activity—in Iceland, for example; at shallow depths where few or no volcanoes are active, as along the San Andreas Fault in California; at a variety of depths along the arcs of islands and deep ocean trenches, mostly in the western Pacific; and at greater depths beneath the continents.

When earthquakes along submarine trenches and island arcs are plotted on a profile cross section of the earth, the resulting pattern shows they have happened on an inclined fault. This makes geologists believe several things about earth tremors: they represent the boundary between two plates; they represent the downthrusting, or dropping away, of the floor of the ocean as one plate rides out over the other; they are a place where either volcanoes are squeezed up from the mantle or the puckering of the earth's crust allows volcanic magma to reach the surface from the mantle.

Most of the earthquakes that take place beneath the continents are recorded along a wide belt of faults stretching across the southern edge of Europe and Asia, where they probably represent old plate boundaries now covered by plates moving up from the south. Some geologists believe that Asia contains as many as fifteen older plates, which were once separate, but are now squeezed together to create the mountains of the Middle East and the Himalayas. Earthquakes in such places can be very severe.

The Pacific coast of South America may also represent this kind of action. Deep ocean trenches lie just off the west coast of South America, directly in front of the great upward thrust of the Andes Mountains. This probably came about because of the collision of two plates, the Pacific and American plates, and the downthrusting of the Pacific plate's eastern boundary. With the movement of the plates, South America's west coast is subjected to many severe earthquakes.

Earth movement can also take place at or near the center of continents, but it is infrequent. One of the most famous of such midcontinental earthquakes took place in the Mississippi Valley in 1811, when one of the most severe tremors in the history of the United States affected a wide area in the center of North America. It has never been repeated in such magnitude.

As in South America, the most frequent and severe earthquakes in North America happen along the west coast. The Pacific Coast of North America is not bordered by a deep ocean trench—although it may once have been. Instead, the chief focus of earthquakes is the San Andreas Fault. The fault may lie over the trench, now covered by the westward push of the American plate. In any event, the upthrust of the Sierra Nevada Mountains seems to indicate the collision of the Pacific and American plates here, too.

Despite all this tectonic activity along the edges of plates, geologists are impressed by the plates' ability to retain their general shape. In contrast to the constant steady movement of the bottom of the sea, the principal outline of the plates seems to have been little altered during the past half billion years. This is probably because the continents rest like great floating islands on the sima of the sea floor. Made as they are of lighter sial, they "float" rather than being dropped or forced back into the mantle. Like logs in a millpond, they jostle about, bumping against one another, as they are moved by the floor of the ocean beneath them.

The analogy of logs in a millpond, however, is more simple than reality. The movement of the plates seems to be very complex and is far from completely understood. Some of what science says about it is speculation and remains to be proved. Even the many cores taken from the sea floor by the *Glomar Challenger* do not prove conclusively that the sea bottom is the chief moving force for change on the surface of the earth.

At the same time, the cores do reveal a great deal about the bottom of the sea. In the Indian Ocean, for example, one of the least studied of the world's seas until recently, the *Glomar Challenger* found a submarine ridge twelve hundred miles long, stretching from the subcontinent of India southward. Cores taken from it show that it once was above the surface of the sea, but that it has since gradually sunk beneath the waves and is now moving toward a nearby trench, there apparently to be carried into the mantle.

Cores taken from the floor of the Gulf of Mexico show deposits of oil and gas at depths far below those previously thought to be the limit of such mineral treasures. Until the voyages of the *Glomar Challenger,* geologists believed such undersea deposits could be found only on the continental shelves. It now seems probable that such deposits are as general under the sea as they are on land.

The *Glomar Challenger* also found widespread deposits on the deep ocean floor of *manganese nodules.* These oddly shaped lumps of ore were previously known to exist on the bottom, but no one knew how abundant they were. Manganese nodules are important, because they contain valuable minerals, including iron, copper, lead, and zinc. Little is known about why they form, but they probably are precipitated from seawater. Large amounts of metals and other minerals are dissolved in the waters of the ocean. Indeed, almost every metal in the Periodic Table of Elements may be present in greater or lesser amounts.

Perhaps the most intriguing and unexpected discovery of the *Glomar Challenger* came as it made its way through the Mediterranean Sea in August, 1970. Midway in that ocean, not far from Italy, the *Glomar Challenger* dropped its drill string to a depth of 6,000 feet and drilled 600 feet into the sea bottom.

Scientists had been expecting to reach a layer of rock at this depth. To their surprise, however, the core barrel brought up layers of sand and gravel. Sand and gravel are unusual on the sea bottom, especially far from land. This particular sample was even more unusual. It contained different kinds of gravel, none of them apparently from any of the surrounding continents.

The mystery deepened when the teeth of the drill bit was found to contain pieces of anhydrite. Anhydrite is a mineral left when brine (water saturated with salt) evaporates. Thus, the bottom of the middle of the Mediterranean not only contained gravel, there were also signs that it had once been the site of a very thick salt-and-water mixture. The thickness of the mineral layer was equal to that around the Dead Sea in Israel, a landlocked lake with no exit.

From this and other later geologic studies, two scientists on board the *Glomar Challenger,* William B. F. Ryan of the Lamont-Doherty Geological Observatory and Kenneth J. Hsü, a Swiss geologist of Chinese extraction, have been able to reconstruct a fascinating history for the Mediterranean. Six million years ago, they say, the Strait of Gibraltar, the narrow passage between the Mediterranean and the Atlantic Ocean—and also between Africa and Europe—was blocked, either by an uplifting of land or a change in the level of the Atlantic, perhaps because of the coming of an ice age. Whatever happened, the Atlantic no longer sent its waters into the Mediterranean Basin. As a result, the sea east of the Strait of Gibraltar gradually dried up. Its waters became more and more salty and finally disappeared completely, leaving only a thick layer of salt on the floor of a deep desert basin.

Half a million years later, however, either the level of the Atlantic rose again or the strait subsided, and the ocean once more poured back into the basin. This produced a giant waterfall, probably one of the greatest falls of water the world has ever seen. For more than a hundred years, ten thousand cubic miles of water poured over the fall each year, a fall of water a thousand times greater than that which annually passes over Niagara Falls. Finally, the Mediterranean again reached the level of the Atlantic and its present size and shape.

Before all these dramatic events, Drs. Ryan and Hsü say, the Mediterranean was probably a series of freshwater lakes, somewhat like the Great Lakes of North America, fed by a giant lake to the north in Europe. This body of water, called Lac Mer by French geologists, once covered large parts of eastern Europe and central Asia, but gradually disappeared before the Mediterranean became a major sea. Lac Mer also contributed to the bodies of water we now call the Black, Aral, and Caspian seas.

The Antarctic is another region where the *Glomar Challenger* has made extensive explorations of the deep sea and turned up many new bits of information. Drilling in the ocean around the Antarctic continent reveals that its lands have been covered and depressed by the polar ice cap for at least 20 million years, longer than had previously been estimated.

Cores also indicate that about 5 million years ago the ice cap at the South Pole extended over a greater area than it now does. Today a few places on the edge of the continent are free of ice during the Antarctic summers. Five million years ago, however, the ice extended two or three hundred miles farther north. As with earlier ice ages, the reasons for this change in climate are not known.

Drilling studies around Antarctica and in the ocean near New Zealand and Australia show that these two island landmasses were once part of the south polar continent. About 80 million years ago New Zealand broke off from Antarctica and began to move northward to its present position, its rigid plate sliding over the slippery mantle beneath. Not long afterward Australia, which had also been attached to Antarctica, broke away and began to move northward. It is still moving slowly toward Asia and may, in another 50 million years, push against Southeast Asia, as India is now doing.

In July, 1974, the announcement came that while the *Glomar Challenger,* with a multinational scientific team aboard, was probing the ocean in the South Atlantic east of the Falkland Islands, the drill bit into rock 1,835 feet below the sediment and brought up a core that proved the theory that South America and Africa were once joined. The sea bottom in the South Atlantic is no more than 130 million years old, yet the core sample was identified as 600-million-year-old granite, a part of the continental shelf projecting eastward from South America.

Like a piece in a jigsaw puzzle, this projection of the Falkland plateau would fit almost perfectly into the indentation of the Mozambique plateau off Durban, South Africa, 1,600 miles away. Thus still more evidence for the theory of continental drift has been provided.

The *Glomar Challenger*'s cores from the Caribbean Sea have revealed some new facts about this part of the world too. The Caribbean plate seems once to have been "masked"

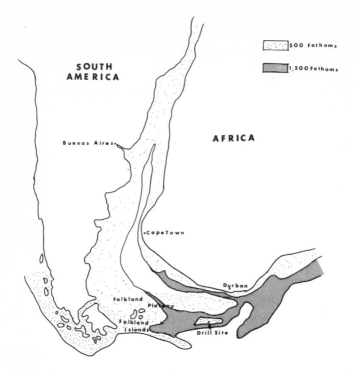

500 Fathoms

1,500 Fathoms

SOUTH AMERICA

AFRICA

Buenos Aires

Cape Town

Durban

Falkland Plateau

Falkland Islands

Drill Site

Map of the "missing link" between Africa and South America discovered by the *Glomar Challenger* in drilling into basement rock in the ocean bottom off the Falkland Islands. The map shows how the two continents must have looked when they were much closer together. Drawing is based on a *Time* magazine map.

by Africa and South America. As the two continents parted and were pushed away from one another by sea-floor spreading along the Mid-Atlantic Ridge, the Antilles, the islands of the Caribbean, were exposed and pulled apart from one another. The result was the Panamanian Basin, which lies in the Caribbean off the coast of the Isthmus of Panama.

The Panamanian Basin has a very high rate of sedimentation. About five inches of sea sediments rain down on its floor every thousand years. This high rate of deposition probably happens because the basin is near the equator, where sea life is most abundant. Micropaleontologists in the future may find the deep layers of sediments of value in establishing dates in the past.

The same fossil record may also be of value to scientists interested in the evolution of life. The study of microfossils, when added to the study of fossils found on land, may help to tell more about when and the way in which the continents separated from one another.

Land fossil records used for this purpose are divided into four categories: *convergence, divergence, complementarity distribution,* and *disjunct endemism. Convergence* seems to have taken place when the continents were joined together early in the earth's history. The fact that the continents were touching allowed many land creatures to migrate far from their original homes. For example, mammals of North America migrated south to South America across the Isthmus of Panama late in the development of life on earth.

Before this time North and South America were separated by water, and the Isthmus was submerged beneath the ocean. In such circumstances species on two continents tended to *diverge,* developing differently, although still bearing some resemblance to one another.

In *complementarity* development, both land and sea species tend to evolve in relation to the location of continents. If continental masses separate, marine fossils tend to become similar, because they are able to move through the sea and be near one another. Land species, on the other hand, tend to evolve divergently. If the landmasses later slid together, the marine species would evolve differently while the land species would be similar.

In *disjunct endemism* fossils found in widely separated parts of the world may be much alike. For example, the fossils of certain kinds of dinosaurs found in the United States and eastern Africa are quite similar. They apparently were separated from one another for millions of years, yet continued to evolve along similar lines. Although the exact reasons are not known, this probably happens because the species originally came from the same place, moved to areas on two continents that were similar in environment and then continued to evolve along similar lines, even though they were separated by both land and sea.

The chief advantage of these classifications, so far as marine geology is concerned, is the light they throw on the separation and movement of the continents, which were all once part of the same protocontinent. Marine fossils, of course, tell only a part of the story. To understand the matter completely, it is also necessary to study the fossils and geology of the continents.

Deep-sea fossils help to tell something of the variation in climate that the earth has experienced in the past. Minute sea creatures apparently tend to increase both in number and species during warm intervals in the earth's climate. They are limited in number and species when ice ages appear. Marine fossils also indicate that the earth's climate has had some effect on the evolution of life. During warm periods evolution seems to have been speeded up. During cold periods it has tended to slow down.

Variations in climate are measured through the examination of cores taken by the *Glomar Challenger*. Variations in the right- and left-handed curls of the shells of *Globorotalia truncatulinoides* and *Globigerina pachyderma* in core samples seem to be found in parts of the ocean floor where the temperature of undersea currents has varied from warm to cool. By mapping the location of core samples showing that warm-water creatures have been deposited on the ocean floor, scientists can get an idea of the extent of warm waters during different periods in the past. Samples of *Glomar Challenger*'s cores show, for example, that the Atlantic's waters have been both warmer and colder in the past and that they have extended over varying parts of the ocean.

This could mean one of three things: the climate of the earth in general has been warmer; it has been colder; or there have been important changes in the levels at which cold and warm currents of the ocean flow.

If the fossils mean the ocean in general has been colder in the past—not just its currents—then it is possible to date the times when it was colder as the periods of ice ages, when the ocean's waters were turned into ice and the level of the sea was lower. Warmer times, when the ice melted and was even scarcer than it is today, may have been periods during which the level of the seas was much higher.

The warmth or coolness of ocean currents is of particular interest to scientists, for it can have an important effect on the land. Today we know that the Gulf Stream, which flows northward along the Atlantic Coast of the United States and then across the ocean's northern reaches to England and Europe, is an important factor in warming both the American and the European shores. The Japan Current, which passes along the islands of Japan and eventually reaches the west coast of the United States and Canada, has a similar effect.

Apparently, both these currents have varied in the past. Cores containing *Globigerina pachyderma* taken over wide stretches of the Atlantic show that the warm-water species of this marine organism once existed all the way to the North Pole. The present limit of this creature is far to the south. Clearly, the Atlantic floor once was covered by much warmer waters in the past.

This finding further implies that the floor of the Atlantic is young compared to the continents that border it. Why then have its currents changed? Although it is not possible to be specific, the shifting position of the shores of North America and Europe and of South America and Africa must have had their effect on the movement of ocean currents. Not only the upper levels of the ocean, but the lower and bottom currents—which sometimes move in opposite directions—must also have been affected.

The same is true of the currents around Antarctica. Antarctica today is bathed by the Antarctic Circumpolar Current, a vast sweep of water that moves completely around the continent, sending out deep, subsidiary cold currents into every ocean in the world. The Circumpolar Current carries a greater volume of water than any other on earth. Its swift movement also grinds and churns the sea bottom. Yet it probably was not always either so swift or so cold. When New Zealand and Australia were both part of Antarctica, the movement of the current must have been different from what it is today.

To learn more about the current, its past movement, and its present effect on the world ocean, the scientists on the

Glomar Challenger sailed south in 1974 to drill the deep sea bottom along the path of its movement. It may be some time, however, before the cores gathered during this expedition will yield their secrets. The very speed with which the *Glomar Challenger* is gathering material has begun to pose problems in analysis, for the study of the cores is gradually falling behind the numbers being collected.

Like the pieces of the moon brought back to the earth by the astronauts after the voyages of Apollo spacecraft, the cores collected by the *Glomar Challenger* may be examined by any geologist. Indeed, the Deep Sea Drilling Committee recently advertised for scientific applications for core studies. Yet miles of cores remain to be studied.

In part, this is because of the small number of scientists interested in marine geology. In part, too, it may be the result of the Deep Sea Drilling Committee's decision to hold cores for a year before releasing them to general study. Although requests for core samples are increasing, there are still many more samples than requests for their use.

Some scientists have suggested that it would be wise to pause in coring operations to allow studies to catch up with the amount of material available. At present, however, the National Science Foundation and the Deep Sea Drilling Committee plan to continue the *Glomar Challenger* voyages, offering opportunities for more scientists from other countries who wish to serve a leg aboard her.

In this part of the *Glomar Challenger* program, there will be fewer holes, with more cores taken at greater depths below the ocean floor. More attention will also be devoted to the cores already gathered and now available for study.

Dr. Edward L. Winterer (right), of the Scripps Institution of Oceanography, points out ancient rock specimens recovered from deep beneath the floor of the Pacific Ocean to John I. Ewing, of Lamont-Doherty Geological Observatory. Dr. Winterer and Mr. Ewing were cruise co-chief scientists on Leg 17 of the *Glomar Challenger*.   *Courtesy Scripps Institution of Oceanography*

With the exception of the voyage of the first *Challenger* in the nineteenth century, there has never been such a wealth of material for marine geologists to study. Whether important discoveries still lie hidden in the cores taken to date is, of course, unknown, but it is clear that many of the secrets of the ocean bottom remain to be uncovered. They, in turn, will open the way to a new understanding of the world beyond the bottom of the sea.

Chapter 6

WHAT'S IT
GOOD FOR?

There once was a newspaper science reporter who closed every press conference he attended by asking scientists of their latest discovery: "What's it good for?" No matter what the discovery was, he wanted to know its practical value.

"What's it good for?" or "What good will it do us?" are questions scientists are frequently asked, but often they cannot answer such questions accurately. They do not know the practical value of their new knowledge.

Moreover, the final practical value of some scientific discoveries often turns out to be unexpected. Often the final results of scientific knowledge are far removed from the original reasons for which the research was begun. One of the best examples in recent history is the development of nuclear energy.

Scientists first studied the nucleus of the atom because

they wanted to know more about its structure. They had no idea that both the nuclear bomb and the nuclear power plant would result from their curiosity about the nature of matter.

This may be true of the exploration of the bottom of the sea. Marine geologists and oceanographers had no goal in mind other than obtaining knowledge when they began to study the sea floor. They wanted to end man's ignorance about this last earthly frontier, and they wanted to extend the information about the earth's continental crust that they already possessed. They felt they could not understand the latter without knowing more about the former.

What they have found may seem to be of little use to us today. Drilling in the ocean at depths of ten to twelve thousand feet is a technological achievement, but it means little to the average dweller on a continent. We do not see the cores that are returned to the surface; we know little of the minute fossils they contain. They record chronicles of the past so ancient that they are beyond our reckoning.

Why should we, too, be concerned with the bottom of the sea and what lies beyond it? There are two principal reasons. First, the bottom of the sea may have an immediate importance for mankind. The waters and basins of the oceans are our last unexplored and untapped reserve of natural resources.

Secondly, an understanding of the ocean bottom is essential if we are to understand the earth. Without knowing more about the oceans, including their floors, we will never understand how our planet was formed and what its future is likely to be.

The most immediate practical reason for studying the

ocean bottom is simply to know what it is like. Although earlier exploration has filled in the gaps on bathometric charts with most of the seamounts, guyots, rises, ridges, shoals, reefs, and trenches present in the ocean, the voyages of the *Glomar Challenger* have helped to refine this information, giving us a better idea of the appearance of the bottom topographically. Some of this information is of value in sea navigation. Some of it gives us a greater understanding of the deep-sea currents.

More important, the drilling of the *Glomar Challenger* may show the way to new reserves of valuable minerals for man's use. For example, with the ever-increasing demand by our technological society for fuel, we are in constant need of new supplies of petroleum and natural gas. Many of the known oil reserves on the continents are being developed and used; others lie in remote parts of the world.

With most continental petroleum reserves already located, oil exploration has now moved to the continental shelves, and drilling is being carried out offshore in many parts of the world. Some oil has already begun to flow from undersea wells off California and the Gulf states. Undoubtedly, as more pools of petroleum are found along the continental shelves, the deep sea will be explored further. The cores brought to the surface by the *Glomar Challenger* in the Gulf of Mexico indicate that oil does exist at deep ocean depths.

Recently, exploration of the floor of the North Sea off England and Norway has turned up signs of undersea oil. American exploration of the bottom of the ocean off the Atlantic coast of North America shows that there may be deep-sea deposits of oil there, too.

Dr. Maurice Ewing (left), of Lamont Geological Observatory, looks at a piece of oil-laden sedimentary core being held by Dr. J. Lamar Worzel, also of Lamont. The two noted geophysicists were co-chief scientists on the first leg of the Deep Sea Drilling Project. The oil core was recovered in the Gulf of Mexico in 11,743 feet of water, with drill bit penetration 480 feet through the floor of the Gulf. Holding the plastic core container is Jim Dean, who was cruise operations manager aboard the *Glomar Challenger*.

Courtesy Scripps Institution of Oceanography

Inevitably, such discoveries will lead to efforts to exploit further the pools of oil still hidden under the bottom of the sea. Drilling such wells and bringing their oil to land will be hazardous both for the world's seas and for man. The 1969 oil leak in the Santa Barbara Channel off California is an example of what can happen when petroleum is spread over the surface of the sea. Miles of beaches were spoiled, thousands of birds died, and incalculable damage was done to sea life.

At the same time, deep-sea wells require the construction of either undersea pipelines or floating islands capable of serving both as drilling platforms and loading docks for oil tankers. Oil tankers themselves can be a threat to both sea and shore life. The wrecking of the tanker *Torrey Canyon* in 1967 on the coast of England produced results similar to those in the Santa Barbara Channel.

To bring oil to the surface successfully and transport it without spillage will require improvement in both tankers and pipelines, much of it by controls operated from the surface, far from the site of the well. While deep-sea diving vessels are constantly being improved, they do not frequent depths of ten to twelve thousand feet. In addition, methods of both opening and permanently closing wells must be perfected.

All this does not mean that deep-sea oil exploration will not be attempted. Technology is constantly improving the chance of such use of the earth's mineral resources, and it will not be many years before deep-sea oil wells will be commonplace in the world's oceans.

Once the wells are drilled, tankers in great numbers will move in to carry the oil away. Oil pipelines will be lowered to the bottom and oil will be pumped to shore through them. No one knows, of course, how much oil lies beneath the bottom of the oceans, but there is no reason to doubt that it is there or that it will soon be extracted to feed the hungry machines on the earth's surface.

Oil is not the only treasure in the sea floor. The *Glomar Challenger*'s discovery of wide fields of manganese nodules, particularly in the Pacific Ocean, interests mining companies around the world. Three American companies, Summa Corporation, Deepsea Ventures, Inc., and the Kennecott Copper Company, already have begun to study ways in which nodules can be removed from the sea bottom. Japanese and German firms are also at work on ways to mine the deep-sea floor.

Two mining systems are being studied. The first would be a continuous cable to which buckets would be attached. The buckets would be lowered from a ship to the bottom of the ocean. There they would be dragged through the beds of nodules. As the buckets strike the nodules, they are expected to break the nodules off, collect them, and carry them to the ship that is dragging the bucket-lined cable.

A second system would use a kind of giant vacuum cleaner, which would also be dropped to the sea floor behind a ship. The cleaner, which would be mounted on a self-propelled sled, would move over the nodule beds, break the nodules off, and suck the broken pieces up a pipe. Compressed air would be pumped down the pipe to "float" pieces up it to the surface. The undersea cleaner would also screen out pieces too small to be of value.

Many problems remain to be solved before either system will be feasible. Lines and pipes must be sharkproof, and they must be so constructed that they will not become tangled in underwater obstacles. They must also be able to screen out deep-sea sediments that could be disturbed and might clog the mining operation with useless material.

An additional complication is locating beds of nodules of sufficient value. Although nodules cover wide areas of the ocean, their value is not known with certainty. To mine them successfully, they must be assayed.

Finally, ways to refine the metals from the nodules still have not been worked out. The usual methods of removing lead, copper, zinc, and other elements would not work because these metals are so mixed together in the nodules that present mechanical separation systems would be of little value. Smelting, another conventional way of refining metal ores, does not seem practical either. If the nodules are heated in a smelter, an alloy of some or all of the metals is formed, not pure amounts of each substance.

However, chemical separation may prove more successful. It requires dissolving the nodules in acids and then dividing and separating the dissolved metals chemically. The separated, dissolved metals are then precipitated into solids. This method works best for the separation of nickel and copper from the nodules. Additional chemical steps will be required to separate cobalt, iron, and other metals.

Because large amounts of acid are necessary for chemical separation and no large-scale separation plants have yet been built, the cost of this kind of processing is still uncertain. Thus, while it may be practical to separate the metals from the nodules chemically, it may not be economically feasible to do so.

A second chemical process uses ammonia and ammonium

salts. The ore is heated in the presence of carbon monoxide and then treated with ammonia under pressure with more heat. This removes the copper and nickel, leaving iron and other metals behind. A third chemical process uses sulfur dioxide and heat to separate the metals; a fourth process requires crushing the nodules and dissolving them in hydrogen chloride under heat. This makes soluble chlorides of the metals. They are separated chemically and precipitated by electricity into solid metal.

As with the use of acid, none of the latter three ways of separating the nodules into the metals they contain has ever been carried out on a large scale.

Manganese nodules are not the only source of ore in the deep sea. Large areas of the ocean floor are rich in sediments containing phosphorus, an important element that must be contained in the food of all growing things. Without phosphorus, nothing on earth could survive. Most of the phosphorus used in human consumption comes from plant foods people eat or or from meat taken from livestock that have been fed plants containing the element.

Phosphorus has many commercial uses, especially in fertilizers. In the United States alone more than 2 million tons of phosphorus-rich fertilizer is used each year.

Fish and bird droppings (called *guano*), both rich in phosphorus, are sometimes turned into fertilizer. The need for phosphorus-bearing fertilizers is so great because tons of the precious element are washed from the soil by rain each year into rivers and finally into the ocean. There it is distributed over the sea bottom as a kind of grainy sand, as flat slabs, or as nodules, sometimes as much as three feet across.

Mining of these undersea deposits has already begun

close to shore. Dredges scoop up nodules, slabs, and beds of the ore and bring the material to the surface for refining. But such operations have only scratched the surface of the large deposits farther off in the deeper waters of the sea. Methods must yet be worked out to mine these deep ocean beds for fertilizer.

The red clays that cover some of the ocean's abysmal plains may be a source of two other valuable elements— copper and aluminum. Copper, in particular, is in short supply on the continents' crustal surface. Enough of it apparently exists at the bottom of the ocean, according to some experts, to last for thousands of years. Effective methods of removing it, first to the ocean's surface, and then to land for refining, must be devised, however, before it can be of any value.

Lime, diatomite, and several other mineral ores of less importance also exist on the ocean bottom in various places, waiting for the invention of ways to mine them successfully.

Finally, the ocean itself may be a rich source of mineral wealth. The waters of the ocean, as separate from the bottom, contain copper, boron, manganese, uranium, silver, gold, and other important and precious metals. In fact, almost every element known to science probably is present in the seas' waters.

The most common combination of these, sodium chloride, common table salt, is what gives the sea its taste. Salt molecules are composed of equal parts of sodium and chloride. Most of the world's present supply of salt is obtained from deep earth mines or the sea, some of it precipitated in shallow evaporating beds along the shores of the continents.

The ocean also has bromine and magnesium dissolved in it. These elements can be extracted from seawater by chemical and electrical precipitation. In theory, the same processes could be used to remove other valuable minerals from the ocean. Practically, however, very large amounts of water would have to be processed to obtain very small amounts of such elements, and no way has been found to make precipitation economically feasible for many valuable metals. This does not mean that ways will not soon be found to make such mineral riches available in the future.

The ocean may also prove one day to be an almost limitless source of power, if thermonuclear fusion becomes a reality. By fusing hydrogen atoms together to make helium —the same process by which the sun burns—we may convert the water of the oceans into energy.

Hydrogen is abundant in the ocean. Each molecule of water contains one hydrogen atom for each pair of oxygen atoms. Fusion would force hydrogen into helium, and energy would be released by this process. For the process to be successful, however, the hydrogen must be heated at temperatures of millions of degrees. It must then be contained in some kind of a vessel for a brief time before its energy can be used. The great heat of the gas plasma formed at such temperatures exceeds the strength of any known container. Most attempts at thermonuclear fusion therefore have revolved around using lines of magnetic force—efforts carried on so far without success. The lines are rapidly deformed, and the magnetic "bottles" created quickly "leak" before they reach a critical temperature.

If fusion is ever successful, however, thermonuclear plants positioned along the shores of the continents could use the oceans' waters to generate electricity for thousands of years.

Even if thermonuclear fusion is successful, even if the mineral riches of the sea become available through new methods of precipitation, man faces a race between the use of the oceans' waters and his increasing pollution of the seas.

The very vastness of the oceans has given us a false sense of security. We tend to believe the sea and the sea bottom are limitless resources, with an immensity so great it equals that of space. Unfortunately, this is not true. For centuries man has indiscriminately dumped things into the oceans, as if they were a sink without a bottom where all unwanted wastes could be deposited without regard for the future.

Man has also tended to consider the seas a limitless source of food. This assumption is also incorrect.

Although the oceans cover most of the planet's surface, the number of human beings on the continents is large and growing. If the world's population is not checked, if the indiscriminate use of the oceans as a garbage dump is not halted, we may soon reach the limit of the seas' ability to be both a food reserve and a waste disposal ground.

Believing the ocean to be an "endless" resource, we have tossed into it raw sewage, garbage, old street cars, automobiles, the radioactive wastes of nuclear weapons factories, chemicals, and other liquid and solid contaminants. Pollution has become so widespread that a few years ago the oceanic explorer Thor Heyerdahl found human garbage floating in the middle of the Atlantic, when he crossed from Africa to South America in the reed boat the *Ra II*.

But the problem is not solely one of garbage. Increased drilling for oil offshore, the need to carry more and more petroleum and gasoline across the oceans, the location of oil refineries along seacoasts—all have added to the growing threat to the sea and its bottom from oil spills. Crude oil spilled on land is contained by the land itself, but its gummy slime spreads over the ocean surface. Mixed with seawater, spilled oil can contaminate the seas' shores, kill sea life and seabirds, and disrupt the normal food chains upon which man is dependent.

Nevertheless, because of the world's growing shortage of energy, both the drilling for oil and its transportation over the seas is likely to increase, rather than diminish.

Even more problems would be created in any major thermonuclear war. Vast areas of the sea might well be contaminated, perhaps for centuries, by the fallout from nuclear weapons.

Although waste, pollution, and warfare all take place on the surface of the ocean, the bottom of the sea ultimately comes to hold all that they represent in danger to our planet.

The bottom of the sea is as much a part of our home as are the continents. Until recently it has been a part of our planet about which we knew little. Fortunately, our knowledge of it is growing rapidly, and so is our understanding of its value to us. Beyond the bottom of the sea is our planet itself. Beyond the sea's bottom too, is our future. To know the latter, we must respect the former. Perhaps that is the ultimate secret of the bottom of the sea.

Chapter 7

BEYOND THE BOTTOM
OF THE SEA

Because this book is about the bottom of the sea, it has not discussed in any detail the life or contents of the oceans' waters or the events that take place there. That is a subject for another book. Instead, it has been necessary to examine the sea floor as if the ocean above it did not exist, as if it were somehow possible to evaporate the water, leaving just the bottom with its geologic features exposed to view.

Yet the oceans do cover the sea floor. They are an inseparable part of it. Because they are, we who live on the continents all too often tend to think of the ocean only in terms of its surface, without considering the bottom. When we do realize the sea has a floor, we tend not to remember that most of the earth lies beyond it.

Yet it is impossible to separate any of these things from one another. In any consideration of the bottom of the sea, we must also ask: What lies beyond it? What *are* the oceans? Why and how did they come into being? Why does the earth have them? Such questions are a part of the geologic history of the earth, the whole earth, a story now known to be far more complex and longer in time than once was supposed.

Until two hundred years ago men had assumed that the earth and the oceans were much younger than they are. They thought the age of the earth was equal to the length of man's time upon it, largely because they assumed the story of creation recounted in the opening chapters of the Bible to be historically true. Archbishop James Ussher of England, for instance, was convinced that the Bible was literally true, and using various biblical clues, he concluded that the earth had been formed on Sunday, October 24, 4004 B.C. (We now know that this date does not even extend back to the beginning of recorded civilization.)

Questions about such views of the earth's age were first seriously raised in the middle of the eighteenth century, and then some incorrect assumptions were made. The first was made by a German, A. G. Werner, a university professor of geology with wide influence in education. Werner taught his pupils that the earth had once been covered with water, but that this primal ocean had gradually receded. He was not clear as to exactly how this had happened.

The recession of the primal sea, Werner said, left the continents exposed. This was followed by the beginning of tectonic forces, which creased, squeezed, folded, and otherwise changed the surface of the continents. Not much was known about the sea bottom in Werner's time, but it was generally assumed to have followed the same historical process of development as the continents. If anything, so Werner taught, the sea floor was probably older than the surface of the continents. Werner did not wrestle with the problem of geologic time, and his views remained unchanged throughout his life, even though supported by no direct experimental evidence.

In the end, of course, neither Werner nor Archbishop Ussher proved to be correct. Instead, a Scottish doctor, who spent much of his life farming, successfully solved the problem of the earth's age and, in the process, threw some light on the question of how the oceans came to be formed. James Hutton became interested in geology as a hobby while tilling his farm. As he walked over the land, he observed geologic features. Looking at them, he could see that they had been laid down in layers, or beds, but that the beds had been folded, uplifted, and moved about. From such evidence, he concluded that the earth's surface had been volcanic at its beginning, not, as Werner suggested, covered with water. What is more important, he also pointed out that the earth must be far older than Archbishop Ussher or anyone else had supposed. In fact, Hutton finally decided that the earth was so old as to be almost infinite in age.

Hutton also guessed (incorrectly) that the bottom of the sea must be very old, too, an assumption based on his observations of the land. He could not know what we do today, that the bottom of the oceans is much younger than the rock of the continents.

Despite their errors, we should not deal too harshly with Werner and Archbishop Ussher. Neither they nor Hutton had any conception of the age of life on this planet. It would be another hundred years before the English naturalist Charles Darwin, using Hutton's theories about the age of the earth, would publish the theory of evolution of life. Like Hutton, he would finally decide that life, too, was almost infinite in age, but he would add that man had been a very recent result of the evolution of such life.

Hutton's theories were contained in a book and later popularized in a second work by his longtime friend, John Playfair, another Scot. Eventually, these theories came to be accepted as the foundation of modern geology.

Today we know from much experimental evidence that the oldest rocks on the continents are immensely ancient, so old as to be almost beyond our comprehension. These ancient rock beds, which are probably about 3.5 billion years in age, are found near the centers of the continents, for reasons not yet understood.

Most of us will never see these ancient markers of the past. They lie in remote parts of Canada near Hudson Bay and in East Africa. But slightly younger rocks—younger by about a billion years—lie at the bottom of the Grand Canyon of the Colorado River in North America. For millions of years the river has worn its way down through successive layers of rock as the earth has been uplifted beneath the swift stream. Today, as one climbs down the canyon walls, one passes through progressively older and older layers of rock until, at the very bottom, lie the twisted and curled volcanic rocks of 2.5 billion years ago.

Unfortunately, no known continental rocks date back to the time before 3.5 billion years ago, and hence we have no remains of the very ancient earth to examine. Scientists once hoped that the bottom of the seas might contain such material, but now we know that the sea floor is only a few million, not billion, years in age. Any earlier clues to the earth's past seem to have long since been swallowed up by the mantle and recycled into the earth's deep core.

Marine geologists do have some clues about the floor of the sea, however. They believe it can be generally divided into three layers. The first layer probably is either sediment or sedimentary in composition. Beneath it is a layer of some hard substance, perhaps chert. Beyond that is "basement" rock, the oldest and least studied. Probably, however, it is either *basalt* or *andesite,* both of which are volcanic in origin.

The difference in basement rock in different parts of the world remains a puzzle to geologists. Basalt apparently covers large parts of the ocean floor beneath the first and second layers, but andesite, named for the Andes Mountains in South America, also is widespread. There is, in fact, an *andesite line* extending north and south about two thousand miles west of the Asian mainland in the western Pacific. To the west of the line, the basement layer of the ocean floor is andesite; to the east, it is basalt.

The line roughly parallels the deep ocean trenches in that part of the Pacific and seems to mark the place where two plates meet, the Asian and Pacific plates. It may also be a place where the bottom of the ocean is disappearing beneath a plate into the mantle.

The difference between andesite and basalt raises other questions, also as yet unanswered: How does volcanic magma reach the surface of the crust and where does it come from? Is it from the mantle or from the crust?

The difference between basalt and andesite, both volcanic in origin, has led some scientists to believe magma may be made both in the crust and in the mantle. Andesite may be contained in pockets in the crust that have drifted upward from the mantle to be released at shallow depths beneath the surface. Basalt, on the other hand, may be formed in the mantle and may reach the surface through long conduits, which reach through the crust to its surface. The Hawaiian Islands, made of basaltic rocks, may be an example of this kind of volcanic activity, but no one knows with certainty that this is what is happening. Clearly, however, the bottom of the bottom of the sea, the basement layer, may be formed in different ways at different places over the face of the earth.

Answers to some of these questions may be supplied by future voyages of the *Glomar Challenger*. The ship and its scientific crew may also address four other questions on later legs:

Why are the continents so much older than the ocean basins?

How were the ocean basins first formed?

Why have they changed so much more rapidly than the continents?

Why have the continents broken apart?

Fifty years ago scientists thought they might find answers to some of these questions during the exploration of the moon, earth's nearest neighbor in space. Little was known about the moon then, and a theory, since discarded, was that the moon had been formed by being torn from the earth and hurled into space. The gap left on the earth's surface by this great event—so the theory went—was the Pacific Ocean. If this were true, the moon should be made of the same materials as the earth, fossilized in space and available for examination by the first astronaut to land upon it.

Even fifty years ago, however, the moon was recognized as a unique heavenly body. It has no atmosphere, contains no water, and is covered with millions of craters, ranging in size from a few inches to more than a hundred miles in diameter. Because the moon has neither wind nor water, its surface has not been altered by erosion, as has that of the earth. It should be the same, in some places, as it was billions of years ago.

Yet even before the flights of the first Apollo astronauts, scientists already had begun to discard the theory that the moon had been formed from a part of the earth, and the Apollo explorations made this even more clear. The surface of the moon is very old, but there is no certain evidence that it is as the earth once was. Nor does any evidence exist to prove that the moon was pulled from the earth and rolled into its present shape.

Instead, it seems more likely that the moon was created at the same time as the earth, probably in the same manner, but even this is not completely established. The moon contains far less iron than does the earth. It cannot have the same kind of core as does our planet. It has almost no tectonic activity. Few moonquakes have been recorded by measuring devices left behind by astronauts.

Although the moon is less dense than the earth, its crust is considerably thicker. The moon also is offset, so that its center of mass is nearer the earth than its center, perhaps because of gravitational attraction from its nearest neighbor in space. Finally, the moon seems to have never contained any water, certainly never enough to create an ocean or even a small lake. The great, flat, dusty plains called *mare* were mistakenly taken for seas by early astronomers, but they cannot have been created by water. The moon seems never to have captured water or an atmosphere, never to have been home to any kind of life (except astronauts), and it is not a model by which man can understand the formation of the earth's oceans.

If man looks elsewhere in the solar system, he finds little

The moon in one of the most striking photographs ever taken from earth. The moon's maria, its dark "seas" that confused early astronomers, are easily identifiable in this picture.

Courtesy Lick Observatory

else to help him understand the formation of the oceans. The solar system can be divided into three parts: (1) the sun, its center, (2) the inner planets, and (3) the outer planets. The inner planets—the earth, Mercury, Mars, and Venus—are closest to the sun. They are cooler than the sun, are quite small (as compared to the sun and the outer planets), and hard. The outer planets, with the exception of Pluto, are much larger and colder, and they seem to be covered with thick atmospheres of dense, cold gases. Whether or not they contain water, either as a liquid or as ice, is uncertain, but unlikely.

Of the inner planets, only the earth is certain to have water. Mars may have once had water on its surface, but the question cannot be answered with any certainty. Photographs taken of Mars seem to show dry stream beds and the effects of water erosion, but earth scientists and astronomers remain in doubt about whether the planet once contained liquid water. It seems to have none at present. A final determination of Martian water must wait for either manned or unmanned landings on its surface.

Thus, in searching for the beginning of oceans on earth, man is confined to his own planet. He can gather some knowledge from the stars, however, and from this knowledge a theory about how the oceans came to be.

Very probably, like other stars, the sun was formed when gravitational attraction condensed a much larger cloud of hydrogen gas and, through the thermonuclear process, set it afire, converting hydrogen into helium. The sun then was larger than it is today. It spun very rapidly because of the large amount of angular momentum needed to hold its turning mass together. To achieve a smaller size and a slower rotation, the sun had to throw off some of its mass. As it did this, the matter lost from the sun spun in space around its equator. Much of it was lost into space, but a small amount of it condensed into the planets.

Because of its closeness to the sun, most of the condensed material from near the sun's equator went to the inner planets. Some was retained by the outer planets. The condensing matter cooled rapidly, collided with itself, was compacted together (much as a snowball grows in size as it is rolled downhill through the snow), and finally achieved the shapes we know today. The last large bits of material that crashed on the planetary surfaces made the impact craters now found on the moon, Mars, Mercury, and perhaps Venus. Very probably similar craters were also made on the earth, but if so, they have long since been so modified by erosion that they can no longer be seen.

The cooling elements around the earth began to form into water vapor. In this early stage of its life, the earth was much hotter than it is today, and its surface probably was still greatly affected by volcanic action. Gradually, however, the earth cooled; the water vapor turned into rain and began to fall. Rain fell for millions of years, gradually filling the ocean basins (perhaps impact craters) and forming the cradle in which life eventually was to evolve.

With the beginning of the oceans, the long train of geologic events recorded in the oldest rocks became fixed. Volcanic activity and tectonic forces slowed down (but did not cease), and the earth became a stable planet. The oceans, or perhaps a single ocean, covered the face of the earth, and for reasons not known, there may have been only a single protocontinent.

Much has happened to the surface of the earth since then. We know that the bottom of the sea is not static; that even more than the surface of the continents, it has been subjected to constant change; and that it will continue to change in the epochs, eras, and eons of time that lie in the future. Although we know the general outlines of the oceans' development since they were formed, and although we understand much about how the bottom of the sea is being moved about and recycled back into the earth's mantle, much remains to be made clear.

Will the continents continue to drift? Will the earth's core retain its heat? If the earth grows cold, will the continents no longer be mobile? What will this mean for the earth's surface?

All these, obviously, are questions for which there are no easy answers. They constitute some of the goals of a branch of science called *geodynamics,* the study of the forces that create geologic change.

The study of geodynamics began in the nineteenth century in some countries. In the present century scientists have come to realize that it is a worldwide international problem. As such, it is now being considered by the Geodynamics Project, a program of research coordinated by the Interunion Commission on Geodynamics, a body established by the International Council of Scientific Unions. The American branch of this effort is being prepared by the United States Geodynamics Committee, a part of the National Academy of Sciences.

In 1973 this committee published a report entitled "The U. S. Program for the Geodynamics Project," which outlines what the American group believes this country's share of such a plan should be. Included in the report is a series of recommendations, several of which are concerned with the future exploration of the bottom of the sea.

For example, the report proposes that a detailed study of the Mid-Atlantic Ridge be made in cooperation with France. It also suggests that the Deep Sea Drilling Project and the voyages of the *Glomar Challenger* be extended and expanded beyond their present limit—specifically that the *Glomar Challenger* drill deeper holes in the ocean bottom to learn more about the ocean floor's first, second, and third layers. Such holes are to be drilled by the *Glomar Challenger* by 1981. Present plans call for a penetration of more than a mile into bedrock in the western Atlantic.

The report also proposes that more effort be expanded on exploration of the Moho discontinuity and on the upper levels of the mantle, and suggests that additional geologists and mathematicians be trained to do such work. More studies of the material in volcanic magma are suggested, as is new and additional deep drilling on the continents to see if basement rock also underlies the continental crust.

The largest part of the report is concerned with the theory of plate tectonics and the search for proof of the theory. The report urges additional exploration around the edges of the American plate and more attention to studies of the Caribbean, Antarctic, and Nazca plates.

The Nazca plate, the report points out, is of particular importance, because it is a small plate containing almost all the features of larger plates. It lies off the coast of Central and South America in the eastern Pacific, and is bounded by South America, the Chile Rise, the Cocos plate, and the East Pacific Rise. To be found either within it or adjacent to it, the report says, are examples of sea-floor spreading, a deep submarine trench (the Peru-Chile Trench), the Andes Mountains, at least one fracture zone, beds of deep-sea sediments, and a mid-ocean rise (the East Pacific Rise).

The report contends that studies of the Nazca plate may give geologists a more complete history of how plates came to develop and what happens to them after they have begun their movement. It suggests that some of the information contained in the Nazca plate can be gathered by oceanographic ships such as the *Glomar Challenger,* some by studies on land, and some by measurements of volcanoes, earthquakes, sea sediments, and the flow of heat at the ocean bottom.

The studies, the report says, should be international in nature, involving ships of other nations. They undoubtedly would include the *Glomar Challenger.*

Geologists' interest in the Antarctic plate, the report points out, is heightened by the fact that it is the only plate on earth completely surrounded by undersea ridges that are not accompanied by any submarine trenches. Because Antarctica may be a fragment of the oldest existing part of the earth's crust, it may have rocks within it as old as or older than those found in Canada or Africa.

At the same time, the report notes, the study of Antarctica is made difficult, perhaps impossible, by its polar ice cap, which may be as much as a mile thick in places. The ice makes it difficult to study the continent's topography, but scientists may be able to drill through the ice to reach the rock beneath. Seismic wave measurements, using explosions similar to those employed in petroleum prospecting, may also be a way to examine the Antarctic landmass, the report suggests.

The Geodynamics Project's list of areas for study in the American plate is long and takes up a major portion of the report. Chief places of interest to geologists in North America, the report notes, are the San Andreas Fault, Alaska, the Colorado plateau, the Rocky Mountains, and the Appalachian Mountains of the eastern United States.

The report concludes that it would cost $14 million a year more than the United States now spends on geologic research to pay for the additional studies. By today's standards, this is not a large amount for scientific investigation.

The *Glomar Challenger* has already begun at least one part of the report. Leg 37, a voyage sailed in May, 1974, had as its chief goal a deeper penetration into basement rock under the sea. This is the first of what may be several voyages devoted to attempts to explore volcanic rock underlying the sedimentary layers of the ocean floor. The drilling marks the first time the *Glomar Challenger* has devoted an entire voyage to a single objective. It also required new drills and a new drilling technique not used before.

The site of the drill was three hundred miles south of the Azores in the Atlantic Ocean, where some international cooperation in undersea study was already being conducted by the United States and France.

The French-American cooperative expedition is called FAMOUS (French-American Mid-Ocean Undersea Study). It involves the use of French and American deep-sea diving vehicles and other undersea equipment to explore the deep underwater canyons off the Azores, these islands being one of the places where the Mid-Atlantic Ridge juts above the ocean surface. In 1974, the expedition made more than thirty dives in underwater vessels such as the *Alvin* in an attempt to get a more direct look at the bottom.

During previous summers the expedition lowered cameras and lights to the sea floor to take pictures of sea-floor features. Other equipment has been used to make more accurate bathometric charts of the area.

The FAMOUS program will extend through the summer of 1977 and is one of the first parts of the Geodynamic Commission's report to be put into action. It is hoped that other important recommendations will become reality within the next few years.

The name geodynamics also implies something described elsewhere in this book, the concept that the earth is a great engine, that it possesses a dynamic force of its own, which pushes the plates on its surface about and causes the bottom of the sea to be constantly renewed. It is the nature of this force that interests geologists. Perhaps, as has already been suggested, heat alone, radiating out from the earth's core, drives the engine of the earth. Probably, however, the mechanism is more complex.

The earth is a nearly round ball, but it is not a static object, as a ball resting on a table would be. The earth rotates on its axis. At the same time, it moves around the sun in an eliptical orbit. The earth is affected not only by those forces within it, but by the forces outside it, too. It is affected by the pull of the sun and the moon and, to a lesser degree, by the movement of the other planets in the solar system.

The centrifugal force created by the turning of the earth creates the gravitational attraction that keeps us from flying off its surface into space. This force also must have its effect, in ways not yet understood, on the convection currents moving from the core through the mantle to the crust. Convection currents probably are generated by the core's great heat and pressure, but they may also be affected by the rotation of the earth. If they are, the currents seem remarkably stable. From all the evidence that geologists have been able to gather, the rate at which the sea floor is spreading—a measure of convection current movement—has changed little over millions of years.

This seems to indicate that the earth has been turning at approximately the same rate of speed for a long time. It may mean as well that the movement of the tectonic plates on the earth's surface has been at a very stable speed, for the same force that moves the convection currents makes the plates slide over the mantle.

Other geologic evidence seems to bear this out. Antarctica in particular is worthy of study for more information about the earth's dynamic force. It is a very stable plate. Its landmass seems to have shifted little for hundreds of millions of years. Although New Zealand and Australia have broken from it, its location over the South Pole probably has ensured its being less affected by the earth's rotation than any other part of the earth's crust.

Plates near the equator seem to have been more affected. The fracture zones of the Pacific, running as they do parallel to the equator, have been taken by some marine geologists as a sign that the earth's rotation has created latitudinal cracks in the sea floor. The constant and steady movement apart between the American plate and the European and African plates may also be the result of rotational effects.

Rotation may explain why some plates seem to be drifting away from one another while others are colliding. Just as the American plate is moving westward, so the Asia plate seems to be slipping eastward. Could this, too, be because of the earth's rotation? Geologists can do no more today than speculate.

As with the origin of the oceans, the only place to seek answers to such questions is on the earth itself. Little is known about the interior of the moon, but it seems to be much more static than the earth's core, colder, and lacking in tectonic plates. In addition, the moon's rotation is affected by the earth's gravity. Its period of rotation almost equals that of the earth, so that the same side is always facing us.

Even less is known about the other heavenly bodies in the solar system. Venus seems to be rotating slowly on its axis in a direction opposite to that of the rest of the solar system. Mercury's rotation is keyed to that of the sun, and it is very hot on one side and very cold on the other. Information about Mars also is meager, but it may have a hot core. Without direct observations on its surface, however, we are unlikely to know whether it has anything resembling tectonic plates. It may well be, like the moon, tectonically inactive.

Thus, to learn more about the forces that drive the earth, geologists will have to continue to probe the crust of the continents and the floor of the seas. To do so is literally only scratching the earth's surface.

The mantle and the inner and outer cores of our planet make up vastly greater parts of the earth than its crust. Very probably, however, man will never be able to probe the greater part of his world directly. Instead, as he has in the past, he will have to depend on indirect measurement and examination.

This should not be reason for discouragement. Almost all we know of the universe beyond the earth has come with such study and with the use of optical and radio telescopes. Although we may never go to the center of the earth or reach to the next star beyond the sun, we may still learn much about what they are like.

In the end we may well understand a great deal more about the complex planet on which we live, how it was formed, how it came to reach its present state, and what is likely to happen to it in the future. This knowledge cannot help but satisfy our craving to know all there is to know about our home. It also may have great practical value. Knowledge of the way in which the earth's engine works may make possible the prediction of earthquakes, the discovery of new mineral riches, and other developments impossible to predict today. In this sense, the future of the world lies at the bottom of the sea—and beyond. We must seek it there.

Bibliography

Books

Bascom, Willard, *A Hole at the Bottom of the Sea.* New York, Doubleday, 1961.

Briggs, Peter, *200,000,000 Years Beneath the Sea.* New York, Holt, Rinehart and Winston, 1971.

Continents Adrift, Readings from Scientific American, San Francisco, W. H. Freeman, 1972.

Geichie, Sir Andrew, *The Founders of Geology,* 2nd ed. New York, Dover, 1962.

Greenberg, Daniel, *The Politics of Pure Science.* New York, New American Library, 1967.

Marwin, Ursula B., *Continental Drift, the Evolution of a Concept.* Washington, D. C. Smithsonian Institution Press, 1973.

Marx, Wesley, *The Frail Ocean.* New York, Ballantine Books, 1969.

Shepard, Francis P., *The Earth Beneath the Sea.* New York, Atheneum, 1964.

Yasso, Warren, *Oceanography, A Study of Inner Space.* New York, Holt, Rinehart & Winston, 1965.

Periodicals

Hammond, Allen J., "Deep Sea Drilling, Research Lags Exploration." *Science,* August 3, 1973.
———— "Manganese Nodules, Prospects for Deep Sea Mining." *Science,* February 15, 1974.

Matthews, Samuel W., "This Changing Earth." *National Geographic,* January, 1973.

Metz, William D., "Geodynamics Report, Exploiting the Earth Sciences Revolution." *Science,* February 22, 1974.

INDEX

QE
39
.H42

QE
39
.H42